BRIGHT NOTES

RABBIT, RUN AND RABBIT REDUX BY JOHN UPDIKE

Intelligent Education

Nashville, Tennessee

BRIGHT NOTES: Rabbit, Run and Rabbit Redux
www.BrightNotes.com

No part of this publication may be used or reproduced in any manner whatsoever without written permission, except in the case of brief quotations in critical articles and reviews. For permissions, contact Influence Publishers http://www.influencepublishers.com.

ISBN: 978-1-645422-86-0 (Paperback)
ISBN: 978-1-645422-87-7 (eBook)

Published in accordance with the U.S. Copyright Office Orphan Works and Mass Digitization report of the register of copyrights, June 2015.

Originally published by Monarch Press.
Samuel Beckoff, 1974
2020 Edition published by Influence Publishers.

Interior design by Lapiz Digital Services. Cover Design by Thinkpen Designs.

Printed in the United States of America.

Library of Congress Cataloging-in-Publication Data forthcoming.
Names: Intelligent Education
Title: BRIGHT NOTES: Rabbit, Run and Rabbit Redux
Subject: STU004000 STUDY AIDS / Book Notes

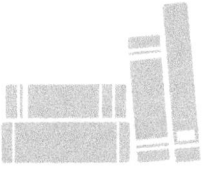

INTRODUCTION TO JOHN UPDIKE

SOME BASIC QUESTIONS

In the *Foreword to Bech: A Book*, Henry Bech admits to his "biographer" (read "creator"), "Withal, something Waspish, theological, scared, and insultingly ironical that derives, my wild surmise is, from you." Bech or Updike - the soft impeachment still applies. Through Bech, Updike expresses some of the envy he feels for those Jewish writers (Bellow, Malamud, Roth, others - but not Mailer!) who can write so uninhibitedly about the gut issues of life; who can philosophize with little or no self-consciousness about the eternal, spiritual problems; and who can shout out the most shocking obscenities without being labeled the hardest of pornographers. From whence (Updike would, one must wildly surmise, dispense with the "from") came such a dispensation?

Critics have referred to Updike's "charming but limited gifts"; to his art as "essentially one of nuance and chiaroscuro"; to the "minor cult" he now enjoys; to his vision as "not only small, for all its brightness; it is even, at times, belittling; it makes people littler than they really are . . ."; to the "small scene" that Updike continues to use as the centerpiece of his literary stage; to the "despair of the daily" (his own phrase) that Updike persists in elaborating upon in his petit point style; etc., etc. Why can't a Protestant, Updike asks, who certainly knows as much about the apocalyptic, find a place among the many Bechs fiddling on the very roofs of the more-Protestant-than-Jewish critics?

Why? He was brought up in a Lutheran home, Updike says, in which everybody did a great deal of laughing and liked to "examine everything for God's fingerprints." An orthodoxy certainly equivalent to the orthodoxy that his eminent Jewish contemporaries had been exposed to. And, as they abandoned their orthodoxy, he did as much when he switched from Lutheranism to Congregationalism. Was it also necessary to have grown up in a "foreign" environment to achieve the proper feeling for human failure? Well, the, Shillington (Olinger) or Mt. Penn (Mt. Judge), and Reading (Brewer) were right smack in the Pennsylvania Dutch section of that state - the scene of his early formative years and the locale for many of his writings. And if he did eventually settle in Ipswich, Massachusetts, why, then, so did his Jewish contemporaries leave their childhood "ghettoes" for more suburban, middle-class environs, once their literary success was assured.

Did Updike suffer as much as a child? His father was a high-school teacher during the Thirties and Forties, when teachers were not quite ready to thumb their noses at the subsistence level. (See the fortunes of young Peter Caldwell in Updike's *The Centaur.*) Well, yes, perhaps that sort of suffering was much too proper for the development of a gut-writer.

But sports-can Updike match Roth's or Malamud's skill in writing about baseball, for example? The record shows an article by Updike on golf (*New York Times Book Review*, 6/10/73), and "First Lunar Invitational" (*The New Yorker*, 2/27/71). True, that ain't baseball; worse yet, Updike plays golf and touch football (and a little poker). Where can one find enough angst in golf, or in touch football?

CONTENTS

1) Introduction to John Updike   1

2) Introduction to Rabbit, Run   17

3) Character Analyses   47

4) Criticism   65

5) Introduction to Rabbit Redux   74

6) Character Analyses   101

7) Essay Questions and Answers   131

8) Bibliography   147

As to the uses of (hard or otherwise) pornography, four-letter words, "liberated" sex, Bellow and Malamud do not qualify for consideration on that point. Roth, however, is a more formidable rival, especially in his very explicit, patently pornographic Portnoy's *Complaint*. In this respect, Updike is no puny challenger. In *Rabbit, Run*, the sex is explicit, even if the language is still too cautious, circuitous, and euphemistic. With *The Centaur*, however, the pornographic situations become more frequent and more obvious, and the language becomes equally more explicit. In *Couples*, Updike has finally joined the vanguard of the post-1964 Berkeley Free Speech movement and the extremely articulate reporters of the wife-swappers, swingers, and bedroom athletes. It remained for *Rabbit Redux* for Updike to abandon forever any inhibitions about the uses and practices of pornography and explicit language. In fact, there are many critics who now feel that Updike has even surpassed Portnoy's *Complaint*. Still, the accolade of completely liberated, modern writer eludes him. Why?

For one, Updike delimits himself. "My subject is the American Protestant small-town middle class," he says. "I like middles. It is in middles that extremes clash, where ambiguity restlessly rules . . ." So, it is the little Wasps, rather than the big Wasps, that he favors (John O'Hara, on the other hand, favored the big Wasps of Pennsylvania, and thereby gained many more readers, both big and little ones.) Then, too, Updike is definitely theologically oriented, something which is bound to confuse, annoy, exasperate, if not totally embarrass, many an average reader, especially the type that helps make up the best-buyer as well as the best-seller list. Furthermore, Updike's genuine flair for **irony** is too often obscured by his "crystalline," well-honed style. Finally, any writer who publicly avers that "An old milk carton is worth a rose" must be suspect. He is too prone to make the tragic trivial and the insignificant heroic. To paraphrase an eminent Elizabethan, Updike believes too often in parvum in multo (too little in a large area).

BACKGROUND AND BIOGRAPHY

John Hoyer Updike was born on March 18, 1932, in Shillington, Pennsylvania, in the general area of Reading. His father was Wesley Russell Updike, a teacher; his mother, Linda Grace Hoyer Updike, an author. He was graduated from Harvard College, A.B. (summa cum laude) in 1954, then spent a year at the Ruskin School of Drawing and Fine Art (Oxford, England) and the two years following as a "Talk of the Town" reporter for *The New Yorker* magazine. Since 1958, he has spent some of his time doing book reviews for that magazine, and most of his time writing light verse, short stories, and novels. He resides in Ipswich, Massachusetts, with his wife, Mary Entwistle Pennington Updike, and their four children: Elizabeth Pennington, David Hoyer, Michael John, and Miranda. He works at a studio on Labor-in-Vain Road in Ipswich, votes Democratic, worships Congregationalist. In 1973 he was working on a play, Buchanan's Dying.

Updike has rejected any attempt to associate his life and family with whatever he writes. However in answer to a statement that his parents seem to turn up quite often in his writing, he insists that his parents should not be equated with any of the fathers and mothers in fiction, and then adds, paradoxically, "But I don't mind admitting that George Caldwell [in *The Centaur*] was assembled from certain vivid gestures and plights characteristic of Wesley Updike . . ." His mother, unlike some of the very middle-class mothers in his stories, is very unmiddle-class, and "an ideally permissive writer's mother."

Harvard was both a happy and a successful experience for Updike. He worked on the staff of the *Lampoon*, doing cartoons, writing light verse, and miscellaneous prose. *The Lampoon* was as ideally permissive as any future ideally permissive writer wanted it to be. At Harvard, he also met Mary Pennington, whom he married in 1953.

Updike's connection with *The New Yorker* may be said to have begun with the subscription he received to that magazine at the age of twelve. He decided then that he wanted to write for that magazine, an ambition that was realized when a poem and a story of his were accepted in June 1954. After graduation from Harvard, he became a staff writer for *The New Yorker*, serving both as a legman and reporter for the "Talk of the Town" section. Such writing, however, had to remain unsigned. (Even E.B. White's many contributions to that department over a period of more than thirty years remained unsigned.) After two years of such writing, Updike left the magazine to become a freelance writer, but maintaining an unofficial connection with it by contributing occasional "Notes and Comments," book reviews, and affording the magazine first call on his poems, short stories, and sundry articles.

CHRONOLOGY OF JOHN UPDIKE

1932

Born in Shillington, Pennsylvania

1945

Family moves to farm near Plowville, Pa.

1950

    Enters Harvard College

1951

    Begins to draw cartoons and write for the *Lampoon*

1953

    Marries Mary Pennington

1954

    Is graduated summa cum laude in English

1954-55

    At Ruskin School of Drawing and Fine Arts (Oxford, England)

1954

    First short story ("Friends from Philadelphia") published in *The New Yorker*

    Three poems ("Duet with Muffled Drums," "Player Piano," "The Clan") published in *The New Yorker*

1955-57

    On the staff of *The New Yorker*

1957

    Moves to Ipswich, Massachusetts

1958

    The Carpentered Hen and Other Tame Creatures (poetry)

1959

    The Poorhouse Fair (novel)

    The Same Door (short stories)

1959

    Guggenheim fellowship in poetry

1960

    Richard and Hinda Rosenthal Award of National Institute of Arts and *Letters for The Poorhouse* Fair

1960

    Rabbit, Run (novel)

1962

    The Magic Flute, with Warren Chappell (Mozart libretto)

    Pigeon Feathers (short stories)

1963

    Telephone Poles and Other Poems

    The Centaur (novel)

1964

    National Book Award for *The Centaur*

    Elected to National Institute of Arts and Letters

1964

    Visits the U.S.S.A. on State Department cultural exchange

    Olinger Stories (a selection)

    The Ring, with Warren Chappell (Wagner libretto for children)

1965

    Assorted Prose (essays)

    Of the Farm (novel)

    A Child's Calendar (juvenile)

    "Dog's Death"

1966

    The Music School (short stories)

Prix de Meilleur Livre Etranger Award for *The Centaur*

1968

Couples (novel)

"Bath After Sailing"

1969

Midpoint, and Other Poems

Film rights for *Couples* purchased by David Wolper

1970

Bech: a Book (novel)

1971

Rabbit Redux (novel)

1973

At work on a play

Publishes long experimental poem in *New York Quarterly* No. 15

LITERARY INFLUENCES

John Updike has been called a maker of fables and parables, but not a philosopher, psychologist, theologian (except by Bech), or organizer of **metaphysical** systems. Still, he has rarely, if ever, been called a pure storyteller, master of the narrative style, or literary experimenter. Moreover, in referring to his work as "meditation, not pontification," he leaves much doubt that the influences upon him have been generally secular and literary. The writers he favors represent a very mixed bag; Salinger, Henry Green, John O'Hara, Nathalie Sarraute, Dante, and Kafka; but also Aristotle, Pascal, Belloc, Kierkegaard, Freud, de Rougemont, Karl Barth, and Niebuhr. His early exposure to Lutheranism had a surprisingly permanent effect on him. "How did the patently vapid and drearily business-like teachings to which I was lightly exposed," he asks, "succeed in branding me with a Cross?" We also don't know how; but the fact is that Christian **imagery** does run through much of his writing. He is intrigued by the mystery-laden universe, and is taken in by a wonder that is more than childlike. It is also highly significant that between the modern theology expressed by the mod Episcopalian minister, Jack Eccles, and the fire-and-brimstone theology expressed by the Lutheran minister, Fritz Kruppenbusch (in *Rabbit, Run*), he seems to prefer the latter's concept of sin and grace.

Updike has very little in common with those contemporary authors (Robert Penn Warren, John Barth, Saul Bellow, for example) who seem to share his willingness as an author to "signal above the heads of the characters" directly to the reader. Warren he can't comment on. Barth seems to be too detached from this planet for his tastes. Bellow he finds too **didactic**. As for the later Salinger and Norman Mailer, he considers them too omnipresent, too self-celebrating.

But Salinger and Nabokov he accepts as mentors, to some extent. Salinger's short stories, by liberating the **genre** from the wise-guy, slice-of-life narrative of the *Thirties and Forties*, "made new room for shapelessness, for life as it is lived," for the kind of milieu in which Updike finds himself most comfortable. Paradoxically, he also has great admiration for Nabokov's ability to create books that are carefully structured.

He envies Henry Green's "sheer transparence of eye and ear," something which he wishes he were able to achieve. The same can be said for some of O'Hara's short stories. (Whether this admiration extends to O'Hara's Pal Joey stories may be doubtful, although in Rabbit Angstrom Updike may have created a consummate heel patently equal to Joey). He also admires the "cool surface" of some of the contemporary French novels, especially those by Nathalie Sarraute. In fact, *The Poorhouse Fair* was intended as an anti-novel, but that may have been a singular exception, in that Updike prefers to describe things "not because their muteness mocks our subjectivity but because they seem to be masks for God."

RELIGIOUS INFLUENCES

"I think of my books not as sermons or directives in a war of ideas," says Updike, "but as objects, with different shapes and textures and the mysteriousness of anything that exists." Be that as it may, there are many sections in Updike's books that are fairly recognizable as lay sermons or sermonettes. The very use of the Pascal pensee as an epigraph for *Rabbit, Run* may be construed as the "text" for the series of sermonettes strewn throughout the novel. Sex and religion can be found in almost all of Updike's writings, and usually in a dialectial relationship. For example, whether it be in Couples or in the two Rabbit novels to be discussed, the problem that seems to concern Updike most is the nature of marriage and the demands made upon it by the social, ethical, and religious dimensions of sex. "Marriage is a sacrament," Jack Eccles, the Episcopal minister in *Rabbit, Run*, declares, and then proceeds to do all he can to bring Janice and Rabbit back together again at the cost of the ultimate tragedy, the death of the baby. And in *Rabbit Redux*, wherein Janice is the "runner," the reader can bet his bottom dollar that the two unfortunate Schussels (fools) will be reconciled.

The sex is there - with all deference paid to Freud and the "new morality" - but even as sex demands of us that we recognize the experience of it as being on a level with the ultimates of love and death (eros and thanatos, according to Freud), religion is demanding to know how these ultimates are to be understood at every moment of our worldly existence. For religion, there is no sex, but love; and that love must be agape rather than eros.

It is, moreover, not just the problem of eros vs. agape, but also the problem of marital vs. extra-marital sex. In his blundering but instinctive fight against the false moralism and the belief that human progress is the ultimate desideratum (even as it is actually concealing the sinful nature of man and society), Rabbit is seeking to develop a more "spiritual" bond with the whore, Ruth, than he now has with his own wife, Janice. He is in fact trying to substitute agape for eros, even as he is running wild like a rabbit in everybody else's cabbage patch.

Man lacks grace, says Updike (agreeing with Niebuhr), because he has retreated from responsibilities into sensuality, and has asserted his individual human independence in pride. Man without grace (Niebuhr again) has the option of turning in either of two directions: He can retreat into his animal nature or to a false faith in his rationality. Rabbit opts for his animal nature, and is credited with being more alive (a dubious distinction, considering the consequences of his actions for everybody else concerned) than the socially responsible people around him.

Why? Because they are seen as rejecting their inner reality for the sake of the phoniness and mass delusions offered by society. But Rabbit, who cannot, or will not, accept any of these mass delusions, may yet be more eligible to receive grace than those other ninety-nine "virtuous" but rational and misguided ones.

Rabbit, however, will not be free of anxiety, for anxiety creates both pride and sensuality. "Man falls into pride," Hamilton paraphrases Niebuhr, "when he seeks to raise his contingent existence to unconditional significance; he falls into sensuality, when he seeks to escape from his unlimited possibilities of freedom, for the perils and responsibilities of self-determination. Rabbit stumbles into both." And is destroyed! When he finally does accept responsibilities in *Rabbit Redux*, he is also destroyed! Rabbit is literally running in circles. Sensuality, which in its purest sense, can be feeling, becomes for him sexuality. His autonomous sex in turn leads him to three significant experiences (in *Rabbit, Run*): sex as shame (175); sex as nothingness (18,73); sex as subconscious experience (240,255). (It is interesting to note at this early point, that sex as a revelatory, mind-expanding experience, does occur in *Rabbit Redux*.)

In short, Updike's main **themes** are difficult to categorize as secular or religious. In the final analysis, they lend themselves more to a religious, even theological, interpretation. They are concerned with the failure of the social institutions in a small Pennsylvania town and with the dual drives of the **protagonist** toward irresponsibility and independence. The two Rabbit novels, in particular, represent a solid Protestant milieu; the characterizations and the implied criticisms of the prevailing Protestant mentality are more often than not reflections or endorsements of Niebuhr's neo-orthodoxy.

INTRODUCTION TO THE "RABBIT" NOVELS

Both *Rabbit, Run* and *Rabbit Redux* are about a "boy of summer" who never grew up. Life had lost its savor for him once he outgrew his glorious adolescent years as a star basketball player. For a while, exaggerated, uninhibited sexual activity satisfactorily substituted for those lost basketball skills. Later, even sex began to lose its appeal for him, and he ran away from wife, family, job, and every other responsibility.

The urge to run, to travel, had always fascinated Harry "Rabbit" Angstrom. As a boy, he imagined that he would be able to travel anywhere and everywhere, occasionally dropping Mom a postcard from some exotic place. Travel, run, move, keep on the go - this was the meaning of life for him. "Yet traveling became an offense in the game he got good at," he observes, toward the end of *Rabbit Redux*. And, in basketball, the penalty for "traveling" is the turning over of the ball to the opposing team, a rule that Rabbit, as good a player as he may have been, must have forgotten.

"A peculiarity of American sexual mores," says Gore Vidal, "is that those men who like to think of themselves as exclusively and triumphantly heterosexual are convinced that the most masculine of all activities is not tending to the sexual needs of women but watching other men play games." Or play games themselves-if they are not too fat by the time they reach their late twenties. At twenty-six (in *Rabbit, Run*), Rabbit Angstrom has run away from his wife and his mistress. Ten years later, when *Rabbit Redux* begins, he is back with his wife and thirteen-year-old son, flabby and resigned to middle-American neutrality, and almost wholly neglectful of his wife's sexual needs. She is in turn driven into the bed of a lover who proceeds to administer to her a remarkably advanced form of sexual education. The ball has been turned over to the opposing team.

The pathetic state of one-time athletic stars, the "boys of summer," is clear enough. During the earlier years of "retirement," the ex-hero is still remembered. He is cheered at alumni reunions, introduced to the crowd before the game or match of the day is to begin, invited to participate in "old-timers games." Then domesticity sets in, also obesity, frequently "ritual drunkenness," or an overactive patriotism evolving from an illogical confusion of an athletic event with a war to defend the national image. It is of course no accident that so many athletic events, especially football games, are so carefully "dressed" in the accountments of military and patriotic usage. But no matter how much the fans may be moved by the magnificently rehearsed maneuvers going on the gridiron, field, or court, there is nothing of any real significance at stake, even for the players themselves: varsity letters, "All-American" accolades, athletic scholarships-it's all make-believe, a sham battle, a "war game" for a war that never really-or almost never really-comes. "True as it is that there is no tragedy without heroic excellence," Arthur Mizener observes, "it is also true that there is none without a significant occasion, and there is nothing significant about a basketball game."

Rabbit Angstrom continues to dream of his lost athletic skills, and expresses his dormant masculinity through a fervent defense of the Vietnam war and a perfervid devotion to God, Gun, and Flag. By the time youth and the New Thought in the form of an eighteen-year-old society run-away, Jill, and black Vietnam veteran, Skeeter, appear, Rabbit is almost ready to have another try at life (and sex), but the "short summer" soon passes, and he is back again in an uneasy, unreal reconciliation with his wife. "The disillusionments of childhood," says William Gass, "can last a lifetime, but the illusions of childhood, carried so far and over such rough terrain only to break like a blister when one has grown up, can embitter and warp a life." Both the athlete and the boy died young, very, very young.

INTRODUCTION TO RABBIT, RUN

THEME AND STRUCTURE: OVERVIEW

The **theme** and structure of the novel are in some measure already suggested in the title. The main character is rabbit-like, that is, inclined to run in all directions, generally easily frightened, highly sexually oriented, and always fearful of being trapped. Harry "Rabbit" Angstrom has had that nickname since childhood; he has also inherited a questionable destiny, if we may analyze his family name: Angst (fear) + Strom (stream) = Angstrom, or "Stream of Fear." (Students will also hear an echo here of the angstrom, a measure of wavelength, one ten-billionth of a meter!)

As a teenager, Rabbit Angstrom becomes a star basketball player, and so literally earns the nickname because of his rabbitlike agility and ability to run. So, for at least his earlier years, everybody is happy to see Rabbit run. But when the high school athlete begins to find adult life one continuous anticlimax after his glorious achievements as an adolescent, then the inclination on his part is to suspect a net or a trap every which way he turns, and that the best thing for him to do, as rabbit or man, is to run. In the course of the novel, Rabbit runs away three times, the first time probably the most meaningful of the three. Rabbit is on his way home from his job as a demonstrator of a kitchen gadget. At twenty-six, the prospect before him is not very bright. His wife is slovenly, pregnant, and inclined to drink. His job is still another one of the dead-end jobs he has been able to get since his discharge from service in the Korean War. His little son Nelson does not seem to have the hands needed to become a good basketball player. His in-laws, the Springers, own four used-car lots in Brewer, and never fail to remind him that their daughter has married beneath her.

On his way home from work on that day in March, Rabbit stops off to play a little basketball with some of the youngsters in his neighborhood. The feel of the ball sets off remembrances of glories past, also a reminder of the hole of unfortunate external circumstances in which he is trapped. When he arrives at home, the sight of his pregnant wife, watching TV with a drink in her hand and no meal being prepared, throws him into a state of despair. She orders him to pick up Nelson at the senior Angstroms' house; instead, he takes off in another direction, hoping to head due south. After driving for some time, he finds that he has been going west, and is actually coming full circle back to where he started his flight. As we shall see later, he meets Ruth Leonard, the big prostitute with a heart of gold, with whom he will try to establish a creative sexual relationship.

The epigraph chosen for *Rabbit, Run* is Pascal's Pensee 507: "The motions of Grace, the hardness of the heart; external circumstances." We already know about some of the external circumstances of Rabbit's life from the brief references to the plot above. We also know how Rabbit looks upon these circumstances as a net or trap (a key **metaphor** in the novel). We shall see how the hardheartedness of many of the characters, but especially Rabbit, turns away from "the motions of Grace," and we shall try to identify those characters later on who, consciously or unconsciously, serve as agents or instruments of divine grace as they appeal to Rabbit. The **theme** of the novel, to reduce it to its most simplistic terms, may be stated as the struggle of a once graceful youth to become a mature, Grace-full adult.

GENESIS OF THE NOVEL

So far as we have been able to ascertain, Updike himself was never a "public" basketball player; nor do we know why he became so preoccupied with basketball in his writings. In any event, much of the general plot outline, **theme**, and characterization of *Rabbit, Run* was tried out in two earlier works: the poem, "Ex-Basketball Player," in *The Carpentered Hen*, and the short story, "Ace in the Hole," in *The Same Door*. In the short story, it's Fred "Ace" Anderson, former star of the Olinger High School basketball team, who has the endless succession of dull jobs, and unlovable wife, a daughter who obviously cannot become a future basketball player, and dreams about his past athletic glory. But Fred is no rabbit type; he is satisfied with his dreams, and eventually even arrives at a meaningful sexual relationship with his own wife. Rabbit, on the other hand, is a captive of his memories of the past and of the visions of escape and freedom that assail him. Rabbit Angstrom runs, and he runs scared.

STRUCTURE OF THE NOVEL

There are three parts (not chapters) to the novel, and in each part a key flight or run by Rabbit occurs. In Part 1, Rabbit takes off at the very beginning of the action (23), when he decides to drive south, instead of driving his son back from his parents' house. In Part 2, the second flight is actually divided between Ruth and Janice. Rabbit has been living with Ruth for about two months, has a job as Mrs. Smith's gardener, and expects to continue that way. Then Eccles calls to inform him that Janice has gone into labor. Rabbit leaves Ruth to go to the hospital. The departure from Ruth is at least a tentative one, knowing Rabbit as one does. The second flight becomes more definitive when Rabbit attempts to make love to Janice soon after her confinement. She refuses him, and he runs off in frustration and anger-to Ruth. Rabbit is with Ruth when the news reaches him that Janice has accidentally drowned the baby. Rabbit comes back (we are now in Part 3) for the funeral and possible reconciliation (at least Eccles hopes for one). It is in Part 3 (at the funeral) that Rabbit disclaims all responsibility for the baby's death, and takes off for the final flight (with a brief stop at Ruth's, for her final rejection of him) for freedom, for nowhere, into space.

The structure of the novel is not really that rigid: nor is it as loose or as sloppy as some more recent novels. It is fluid, it is in-or suggests-motion. "I originally wrote *Rabbit, Run* in the present tense, in a sort of cinematic way," Updike told Jane Howard. "I thought of it as *Rabbit, Run*: A Movie." And to Charles Samuels he explained that "The opening bit of the boys playing basketball was visualized to be taking place under the titles and credits." The effect to be achieved was that of something happening to you at that very moment in which you are sitting there, reading the novel (or watching the film).

The cinematic concept is carried even further in the use of montages, both visual and aural. For example, on the drive down south (or at least he thought he was going south), Rabbit hears over the car radio a melange of popular songs, commercials, and news (29-30). In cinematic terms-or in current TV terms-such a montage could be a mere back-projection conveying the illusion of motion by Rabbit, although he, for all practical purposes, is going nowhere. Other examples of verbal montages may be found throughout the novel.

Another structural device used is the introspective interior monologue, or near-soliloquy, much in the manner of Molly bloom, in James Joyce's *Ulysses*. One is by Ruth (122-24), the other by Janice (208-11), both with very strong sexual overtones. The passages are long, wordy, and in fact violate the principle of fluid or cinematic narration that Updike claimed to be following in writing the novel. The effect might have been stronger - and more consistent with the cinematic principle referred to above - if the first person singular had been used. On the other hand, the author may have intended the "monologues" to be that static in order to suggest the passivity of the two main female characters in relation to the more active Rabbit.

Updike has also made use of the parable or extended metaphor. Because the rabbit **metaphor** is probably the key metaphor of the novel (the trap **metaphor** may be a very close second), it is sometimes hard to differentiate it from the Peter Rabbit story or parable by Beatrix Potter. Although the **allusion** to the Potter story may have been an unconscious recollection on Updike's part, there is a later admission by the author of the parallel between Harry and Peter Rabbit (which we shall explore in greater depth later). Still another parable-or parabolic use of it-may be found in the references by Jack and Lucy Eccles to the Cautionary Verses by Hilaire Belloc. In both instances, the undisciplined Harry Angstrom, the "naughty man," is placed alongside (hence, parable) naughty Peter Rabbit (Potter) and naughty Jim (Belloc).

MAJOR THEMES

"I once played a game real well. I really did, I once played a game real well. I really did, Rabbit tells the minister, Eccles. "And after you're first-rate at something, no matter what, it kind of takes the kick out of being second-rate. And that little thing Janice and I had going, boy, it was really second rate." The "little thing" Rabbit is referring to is his marriage, that same second-rate marriage that Eccles is trying to save. And there was also that one second-rate job after another, and the second-rate 1955 Ford that his father-in-law sold to him in 1957, and his whole second-rate, anti-climactic adulthood following his glorious, free-moving adolescence. This is the main **theme** of the novel-a conscious attempt to reject the "net" of responsibility and an instinctive rejection of the phony, second-rate world around him. The result of this pathetic (not heroic, not tragic) disaffection with life is the powerful impulse to run away-once, twice, three times. The third and last time he runs away, it is the act of a desperate man driven by his instincts, his "feeling" for what is right. It is certainly the act of a coward, and in some ways futile (for he must eventually - and does, in *Rabbit Redux*-come back). But it is at the least a gesture, a token of his desire to continue to fight for life, as the author understands it. "Rabbit, run; it is the author's urgent, ironic advice to his hero, an imperative cry from the heart." Ironically or not, Rabbit's mother echoes the same advice in *Rabbit Redux:* "Run. Leave Brewer. I never knew why you came back. There's nothing here anymore... Don't say no to life, Hassy. Bitterness never helps... Pray for rebirth. Pray for your own rebirth." (175)

Rabbit's life is mirrored in the structure of the book; it is as if his whole life consisted of a series of traps set for him by society. As soon as he escapes from one trap, he blunders into another; life for him seems to be one accident after another, a sequence of grotesque poses assumed to no purpose, "a magic dance empty of belief." While Janice is in the hospital waiting to be delivered of the baby, his doubts become even greater. "There is no God; Janice can die: the two thoughts come at once, in one slow wave." (165) And so he just lived in his skin and didn't give a hoot for the consequences of anything to anybody else. "If you have the guts to be yourself," he proclaims, "other people'll pay your price." (125) But he hasn't got the guts (his sister Mim has, as we find out later), and as Ruth reminds him, "Don't you ever think you're going to have to pay the price?" (122)

If Updike's stories repeatedly support the idea that few if any causes are worth man's sacrifices, and that the age of heroes is long past, then Rabbit, easily disillusioned as he is by a world which he has never made, is right in running. Impulsive as the gesture may be, it is still essential to his spiritual nature. Running, to be sure, makes him a social outcast; he has, after all, rejected his family and all the normal responsibilities which life has imposed upon him. Those rejections, one is led to believe by some literary theologians, are part of his "saintliness." For Rabbit has "sampled conventional ethics and found them wanting." Even Eccles, an ordained minister and theologian in good standing, recognizes some of the attributes of "saintliness" in Rabbit, and agrees that perhaps saints should, after all, not marry. Everybody is eligible for redemption, so long as their hearts have remained open for Grace. (101) And certainly Rabbit, a victim of his instincts, not of his head or heart, qualifies.

Rabbit's angst arises from a fear of nothingness, the consequence of man's having fallen from grace, according to Kierkegaard. Kierkegaard's definition of Existentialism differs from the more popular one given by Heidegger. The latter claimed that man finds meaning only within himself, a definition that Rabbit would gladly live with, if he could; the former claimed that the subjective understanding can be acceptable only when it coincides with "objective truth." Rabbit could find some assurance in Pascal's notion that man "is a creature of contradictions and ambivalences such as pure logic can never grasp," but he could never free himself of the fear of having fallen from grace. And this is the full thrust of the Pascal pensee in relation to the whole novel. Rabbit dreams of founding a "new religion." (234) He conceives of his running as in the nature of a quest, a search in the spirit of Grace. The reader is more inclined to evaluate this running as a product of his fear and irresponsibility, and also of his hardness of heart (e.g., in his reasonable and unreasonable sexual demands upon Janice and Ruth, in his readiness to abandon them and his son Nelson); but he is often soft ("I am lovable," he tells Ruth). He keeps trying to escape from the traps of external circumstances, and, being rabbitlike, he often does. But he never manages to attain that state of grace urged upon him by several "agents of grace": the old farmer at the gas tank, Tothero, the Chief Mouseketeer, Mr. and Mrs. Angstrom, Jack Eccles, Fritz Kruppenbusch, the "Lord's Grace Table Napkins" radio commercial, and others (to be developed below under "Religious Influences"). But Rabbit is not yet ready to found a "new Religion" (the concept is, however, more fully explored by Updike in *Rabbit Redux*), even though he has much in common with Pascal, according to the following passage on the nature of human existence: "When I consider the short duration of my life, swallowed up in the eternity, before and after, the little space which I fill, and even can see, engulfed in the infinite immensity of space of which I am ignorant, and which knows me not, I am frightened, and am astonished being here rather than there, why now rather than then." Or, as our frightened and astonished Rabbit would ask, "Why am I me?" (235) In the context of his character and the circumstances prevailing, he cannot choose to be otherwise. For no matter how hard he may try to be otherwise, he will still be (in the words of Pascal) "an All in relation to Nothingness, a Nothingness in relation to the All."

STYLE: LANGUAGE

In reviewing *Rabbit, Run*, Whitney Balliett said that "John Updike ... writes only for himself. The results of this total self-absorption come very close to the ultimate achieved by all consummate writers-a new prose." Norman Mailer, on the other hand, spoke of the "mud pies in prose" that Updike was guilty of in the same novel. The fact is that Updike's prose is neither; it rarely defies analysis, as does *Ulysses* or *Orlando* (by Virginia Woolf), and can be understood by any reader who makes fair allowance for the occasional poetic flourishes and the long, sustained passages of introspection and recollection, as in the Ruth and Janet "soliloquies" and Harry's visions (especially the one at the conclusion of Part 2). Mailer's reservation (and he had many) is based on (a) Updike's refusal to use real mud in making his pies, and (b) the absence of simple, journalistic prose in a work of fiction.

There are, to be sure, many poetic flourishes in Updike's prose, and we shall give some examples below. There is also a tendency to employ euphemisms in several of the sexual passages, and this, too, we shall illustrate below. The euphemisms are completely abandoned in *Rabbit Redux*, and it is therefore possible to suggest that Updike was trying to reflect the more proper atmosphere of the Eisenhower Fifties in *Rabbit, Run*, as the more explicit language in *Rabbit Redux* reflects the greater permissiveness of the Sixties.

On his way south to the Gulf of Mexico, Rabbit passes through Delaware, the home of the Du Ponts. He begins to imagine "A barefoot Du Pont. Brown legs probably, bitty birdy breasts. Beside a swimming pool in France. Something like money in a naked woman, deep, millions. You think of millions as being white. Sink all the way in softly still lots left." (25) Note the inevitable (for Updike) **alliteration**. But note, also, how appropriate both the language and the **imagery** are for Rabbit. More **alliteration** now, and note, also, the appropriateness of "hot hollow" for a rabbit: "Rabbit rolls in his hot hollow and turns his face to his cool companion, the wall, and through a red cone of consciousness falls asleep." (43) Now a sexual passage, as seen through a very slight film of euphemism: "He returns to her back, until his wrists ache, and flops from astride his mermaid truly weary, as if under a seaspell to sleep." (One can quarrel with the image of Rabbit "astride his mermaid," rather than "astride his sea horse," since in other passages, he does refer to Ruth as his horse.) The final example, also a sexual passage, isn't much more daring, the poet still controlling the lover: "Again, then, they make love, in morning light with cloudy mouths, her tits silky sacs of milk floating shallow on her ridged rib cage. The nipples sunken brown buds. Her bush a froth of tinted metal." The language is not obscene, most of the "questionable" words are right out of folk terminology. In all, Updike's prose manifests the traces one would expect to find in the work of a card-carrying poet engaged in writing fiction.

STYLE: INTERLOCKING IMAGES

There are many symbols, images, motifs, and **metaphors** throughout the novel. Updike's use of "interlocking images" seemed a particularly ingenious and effective device, and the question arose in this writer's mind: How did the effect of a kind of resonance come about? Updike replied that "Some images interlock by chance, others by intent." It is therefore, left to the reader to determine when the "interlocking" is contrived, and when it is fortuitous. Another possible description of this device occurs in Updike's *Bech: A Book*, in which Bech/Updike explains "how in Travel Light he had sought to show people skimming the surface of things with their lives, taking tints from things the way that objects in a still life color one another, and how later he had attempted to place beneath the melody of plot a countermelody of **imagery**, interlocking images which had risen to the top and drowned his story,..." (81; see also 158) Herewith follow some examples of interlocking images.

About Ruth: "Her laugh rings on the street like a handful of change thrown down." To "She laughs again, the coins thrown down,..." (both on 49) "Margaret wriggles at Rabbit's side. She feels somehow like Janice: jumpy." (147) To "Rabbit sits across from them married to this girl he hates." (147) Then back to "'You're just a big clean-living kid, aren't you, you,' Margaret says. She doesn't even know his name yet. God, he hates her." (57) Janice, sitting there, after having come home from the hospital, once again abandoned by Rabbit, "...sits there watching the blank radiance a feeling of some other person standing behind her makes her snap her head around several times." (213) To "Her sense of the third person with them widens enormously, and she knows, knows, while knocks sound at the door, that the worst thing that has ever happened to any woman in the world has happened to her." (220) She has drowned the baby; the third person was death.

The color blue stands for Ruth (see Blue Motif below) and, in the following interlocking image, for guilt: Harry thinks, "Something held him back all day. He tries to think of what it was because whatever it was murdered his daughter. Wanting to see Ruth again was some of it..." (225) Next, "the darkness is mottled with an unsteady network of veins like the net of yellow and blue that mottled the skin of the baby." (230) Then, "His daughter is dead, June gone from him;... never balance her faint weight in his arms again and watch for the blue knives of her eyes..." (242) Finally, of Ruth, "the blue of her eyes is darker." (249)

The finest example of this device is the way in which Updike combines all three of the four main **metaphors** into one: the net or trap, the basketball, and the running metaphors: "He feels his inside as very real suddenly, a pure blank space in the middle of a dense net." (254); "... what to do, where to go,... It's like they heard you were great and put two men on you and no matter which way you turned you bumped into one of them and the only thing to do was pass. So you passed and the ball belonged to the others and your hands were empty and the men on you looked foolish because in effect there was nobody there." (354-5); "...but with an effortless gathering out of a kind of sweet panics growing lighter and quicker and quieter, he runs. Ah: runs. Runs." (255)

SYMBOLISMS

"I do not write in code," says Bech. "I depend upon my reader for a knowledge of the English language and some acquired vocabulary of human experience. My books, I hope, would be unintelligible to baboons or squid. My books are human transactions-flirtations, quarrels." (*Bech: A Book*, 169) In the main, that is true; notwithstanding, to understand and appreciate *Rabbit, Run* fully, the reader must "decode" several of the many symbols that are strewn throughout the book. The colors blue and orange, for example, are such recurrent symbols as to become important motifs (narrative and thematic symbols) and will therefore be treated separately later on. The individual symbols follow.

Mt. Judge

Rabbit's birthplace and home town is Mt. Judge, the town on the east side of the mountain, Mt. Judge. His descent, physical and moral, is down the west face of the mountain to the city of Brewer. Mt. Judge thus becomes "Mt. Judgment."

Song Titles (29)

Some of them are suggestive of Rabbit's anticipation of the pleasures he will enjoy under the "huge, white sun of the south"; others hint strongly of his imminent return to Brewer (not to Mt. Judge).

Right, north (35)

Rabbit's sense of direction betrays him, and he turns instinctively right, north, or away from the forbidden pleasures of the south, the Gulf of Mexico.

"Signs" to return (35)

"Throughout the early morning the music (Cf. 29 above) keeps coming and the signs keep pointing." The trip back is easier. "He wonders why there are so many signs back and so few going down." (36)

Pelligrini (65)

The Italian word for pilgrims is pellegrini. Through some form of literary license (for the substitution of i for e) the author may have intended Rabbit to think of himself as a pilgrim (on a quest), rather than a fugitive.

> "The door snaps shut behind him irrevocably. His key is inside." (84)

He will never return to Janice (at least in this book).

Sunflower (91)

The Sunflower Beer sign, near Ruth's apartment. Orange symbolizes passion, sex. The sign lights up at night, the conventional (?) time for sex.

Fosnacht (105, 110)

German for "fool." Last one down is a ... fool. Peggy Gring is a moron, married to that hick, Morris Fosnacht. Harry will never be a Fosnacht, nor will he have anything to do with Fosnachts-at least until *Rabbit Redux*, when he has a brief affair with Peggy.

Hole (110)

In one connection, it's a golf hole; in a sexual context, his missing the "hole" with his putt ("two or three fucking feet too far") is symbolic of Janice's crucial rejection of his sexual demands.

Bartenders and Embalmers (145)

The juxtaposition of the two foreshadows the drowning of the baby. Janice is a heavy drinker, and will be fairly well smashed when she tries to bathe the infant.

St. Joseph's Hospital (162)

The hospital as "church"; Rabbit runs most of the way to the hospital, to "salvation." Eccles is there, "officiating," offering him a cigarette. "The effect is somehow of a wafer of repentance and Rabbit accepts." (164) Sister Bernard is a nun dressed in blue (Cf. Ruth), the color of Rabbit's adultery.

Dr. Crower (167)

A crow or raven is a classic literary symbol for death. Rabbit is accused of sitting in the hospital "like a buzzard... hoping she's going to die." Back to p. 164: "He is certain that as a consequence of his sin Janice or the baby will die."

Rebecca June Angstrom (182)

The baby's name is a compromise that will not work; the reconciliation is a false one.

Summer Solstice (195)

On Sunday morning, the day before the summer solstice (June 21), Rabbit goes to church. When he returns to Janice, the final and crucial rejection occurs, and the unfortunate drowning of the baby follows. Writes Frazer (*The Golden Bough*, pp. 720-21): "The summer solstice, or Midsummer Day, is the great turning point in the sun's career, when, after climbing higher and higher day by day in the sky, the luminary stops and thenceforth retraces his steps down the heavenly road." Rabbit's progress will henceforth be downward; he will be rejected by both Janice and Ruth; he will run away for the last time.

Shattered Orange-juice Glass (213, 218)

See orange motif below. Janice has rejected Harry's sexual advances; the accident; Harry's brief return.

Two Perfect Disks (234-35)

After the death of the baby, Rabbit has a vivid dream in which he sees the moon eclipsing the sun, "lovely life eclipsed by lovely death." He is excited by the thought that such a revelation is a signal to him to go out and found a new religion. (Eccles has probably worked on Rabbit too long, so that he really considers himself somewhat of a Messiah.) When he awakens, Janice is bending over him, and he realizes "that he has nothing to tell the world." (However, we have to wait until *Rabbit Redux* to see how Updike develops the moon motif.)

Flowerpot Red (249)

Brewer is the color of flowerpot red. It also suggests the flowerpot in the Peter Rabbit story. Brewer is also the strange "cabbage patch" (Ruth lives in Brewer) where Rabbit had cavorted. Note again the great neon sunflower (patterned after the real sign for Sunshine Beer, made in Reading, Pa.) at the center of the city, now looking "small as a daisy."

STYLE: ORANGE MOTIF

Orange is one of the two pervading colors in this novel (blue is the other one). Rabbit wants to go south, to the orange groves, reflecting Updike's awareness of oranges as love-gifts from back in Elizabethan times. Orange-ripe fruit is a symbol for passion. The motif begins with the oranges that Rabbit has to provide for Janice's Old-fashioneds (15), then the girls with orange hair in the roadside coffee shop (31), and Margaret's orange lips in the Chinese restaurant (51). Ruth's face is "caked with orange dust." (51) The "enormous sunflower erected" (63) includes both the color orange and an obvious sexual symbol. Rabbit is taken in by the orange shorts Lucy is wearing (98), especially the "seat of her orange shorts" (99), and he can't help slapping "her sassy fanny" (100), because she suggests to him "a fine-grained Ruth." He may not have reached those orange groves, but the orange groves are still with him in his thoughts.

At the Castanet, Rabbit can't help noticing the colored girl in her orange uniform with the orange frills that swing as she walks. (146) The floor of the cafe is paved with orange tiles. (152) While waiting in the hospital for Janice to be delivered of the baby, he nervously rattles the magazine in such a way that it sounds like orange crates being torn apart (165), a probable symbol of the destruction of the sex between him and Janice, as later events prove to be the case. Rabbit visits Janice in her room after the delivery, and remarks that "you're pretty sexy for somebody in your shape." Janice would like to invite him into bed with her, but the bed is too narrow, and she suddenly has "this terrible thirst for orangeade." (171) Harry (trying to be less of a rabbit) spends that night at the house of the Eccles, and the following morning is served orange juice by Lucy (those orange shorts again?) for breakfast. (173) During the few days after the baby is born, Rabbit spends much time with Nelson, at one time sharing an orange soda with him (187), but "the artificial sweetness fills his heart." (Cf. the orange crates above.)

Rabbit has now left Janice for the last time. (207) She is upset, and takes to drinking again. In making breakfast for herself and Nelson, she smashes an orange-juice glass (213), and later tries to clean up the "orange mess" in the baby's crib. (218) She prepares the bath for the baby, and wishes she could clean up the "orange mess" in her life by getting into the tub with the baby. On a condolence call to the Angstroms, Mrs. Tothero parks her car in front of an orange fire hydrant (233), as if to suggest that water (Cf. Janice at 218) can quench passion. Finally, there is that neon sunflower, now "small as a daisy." (249)

STYLE: BLUE MOTIF

When Rabbit asks Ruth to explain what her relations had been with Harrison and the other men in her life, she replies. "Oh, I don't know, what do you do? You make love, you try to get close to somebody." (155) Rabbit had never been able to get close to anybody but himself, and so Ruth held out a promise for him of some greater experience, some greater truth, perhaps even a different, more spiritual kind of love. The color blue identifies Ruth in this context, and at other times in the context of the guilt that Rabbit feels in his relationship with her.

The first significant reference to blue is in Rabbit's reflection: "Her eyes were that blue. Unflecked. Your heart lifts forever through that black sky." (83) He had met Ruth on Saturday, the day after his abortive flight south. Now it is Palm Sunday, he has returned to his own apartment to get some fresh clothes prior to moving in with Ruth. A neighbor greets him: "...Palm Sunday is always blue. It makes the sap rise in my legs." (85) Now he's on his way: "He feels Ruth, the dishes done, waiting on the other side of the mountain. Blue beyond blue under blue." (86) He is intercepted by Jack Eccles, the Springers' Episcopal minister, whose suit either distracts or disturbs (blue = guilt) him because "It is really blue, a sober but elegant, lightweight, midnight blue." (86) Rabbit has cause to be disturbed, because Eccles does try, ever so subtly, to criticize him for leaving Janice. The reader notes later on that back in his seminary, the rooms were lined with "handsome blue exegetical works." (158)

Rabbit and Ruth decide to walk up Mt. Judge. The gravel bothers Ruth. Harry suggests that she take off her shoes. "These blue stones are stopping." (94) Stones or scruples? Ruth is now pregnant, and Rabbit is slowly becoming aware: "The blue of her irises has deepened inward and darkened with a richness that, singing the truth to his instincts, disturbs him." (122) During their "shacking up," Ruth has had calls from some of her former "clients" (she says about five of them), but Rabbit is satisfied of her loyalty to him. "Like the past was a vine hanging on by just these five shallow roots and it tore away easily, leaving her clean and blue and blank." (146) But now that the baby is a "wrinkled blue corpse" and "the darkness is mottled with an unsteady network of veins like the net of yellow and blue that mottled the skin of his baby" (both at 230), blue=Ruth=guilt. (Cf. also 225) He will never again see the "blue knives" of the baby's eyes (242), the funeral procession moves slowly up a "crunching blue gravel lane," (242-3) and the vista from the cemetery across the valley "looks different, more blue." (243) Rabbit has now taken off on his final flight, "jauntily hanging his blue coat over his shoulder on the hook of one finger, Janice and Eccles and his mother and his sins seem a thousand miles behind." (247) Maybe Ruth will be his final destination. Not even Ruth: "You just wander around with the kiss of death," she tells him. "Get out. Honest to God, Rabbit, just looking at you makes me sick." (251)

STYLE: RABBIT METAPHOR

There is little point in elaborating on the Rabbit **metaphor**; it is a fairly obvious one. However, just a few examples for the record. "So tall, he seems an unlikely rabbit, but the breadth of white face,... and a nervous flutter under his brief nose as he stabs a cigarette into his mouth partially explains the nickname," given to him as a boy. (7) "His upper lip nibbles back from his teeth in self-pleasure." (9) His car is "his locked windowed hutch." (37) At their very first meeting, Ruth remarks, "Well, you're a big bunny." (49) As he disrobes in her apartment, she observes, "In those damned under-clothes you do look kind of like a rabbit," and adds, even more meaningfully, "I thought only kids wore those elastic kind of pants." (71) A little later, she says, fondly, "Oh, my Rabbit ... You just wander, don't you?" (92. Cf. 251 for the **irony** of this remark.) In an argument with Ronnie Harrison, Rabbit becomes quite agitated, and is told, "Harry, now don't wrinkle your nose." (148) Afterwards, Ruth refers to her "gentle rabbit." (156) All of these instances are, of course, mere parameters of the larger, more important Peter Rabbit, the "naughty man" in someone else's "cabbage patch," parable; the moral, rather than the merely physical, implications of the total metaphor.

STYLE: TRAP METAPHOR

On the way out of his apartment to pick up Nelson, "Rabbit freezes, standing looking at his faint yellow shadow on the white door that leads to the hall, and senses he is in a trap."

(16-17) Janice, Nelson, family, job, dead-end existence-everything is a trap, and he must find a way to evade it. He tries to escape to the Gulf of Mexico, and loses his way. "The more he drives the more the region resembles the country around Mt. Judge ... Indeed the net seems thicker now." (32) The red and blue lines of the road map conspire against him, the map is a net he is caught in. (34) He is running, but like a mechanical rabbit pursued by greyhounds on a dog track. The night is fading, and back home there is "a net of telephone calls ... strings of words, white worried threads shuttled through the night ..." (37) Ruth invites him into her bed for the first time, and he senses a trap-she may use a diaphragm while he is not looking. (67) But he eventually prevails, and the experience is both satisfying and exhausting; moreover, he knows that he is "heading into the center of the net," and wants to, because this time there may be a chance to rest. (82) He knows why Eccles has approached him - the objective is to bring him back to Janice. "The trap is there waiting; damn him, he's so sure I'll come down the path." (105) Ruth and Rabbit join Margaret and Ronnie at the Castanet Cafe: who's setting the trap this time-Margaret, who reminds him so much of Janice? (146) The night before Janice is to come home from the hospital, Rabbit sleeps in his own apartment. The wrinkled bed reminds him of a net, but he lies down on it nevertheless. (194) The death of the baby might have been averted if he had agreed with Janice's refusal to have intercourse with him and had not run away. She was right, he was wrong, but he couldn't stand being cooped up, feeling locked in, "in this damn hole all day." (207, 225) The baby was a net or trap of sorts (230), but he's willing to accept the blame for her death. He'll speak to the coroner because for once in his life he wants to be locked in place. (238) The net of law is synonymous to him with the only kind of orderly existence he was ever happy with-sports and games, all played according to strict rules. Basketball was the only meaningful aspect of his former, present existence.

STYLE: BASKETBALL METAPHOR

Rabbit is elated when the boys in the street let him try a few shots at the basket. "That his touch still lives in his hands elates him." (9) Basketball symbolizes youth for him. The skimpy uniform, the running, the freedom, the ability to elude the guards-all this is possible in a game, but not in life, at least not for the adult. As an adult, sex has come to symbolize basketball (and youth). Sex, to Rabbit, is so much like playing basketball. By reversing the usual order (basketball symbolizing sex), sex will now be symbolizing basketball, and Rabbit will be trying to recapture some of his basketball skills through sexual activities. (See section below on Sexuality).

The route Rabbit chooses in going south will not be along the water; he will proceed right down the middle (as down the middle of the basketball court), "right down the broad soft belly of the land" (straight for the basket, the "hole," the vagina). (30) The basket was "the high perfect hole with its pretty skirt of net." (35) That was his youth, when a Saturday morning sky was "the blank scoreboard of a long game about to begin." (37) (Cf. also that Saturday morning in March when his first flight began.) In excited conversation with Eccles, Rabbit lifts his hands and jiggles them "as if thoughts were basketballs . . ." (107) At the reunion with Ronnie Harrison, an old teammate, Ronnie addresses Rabbit as "Ace," (Cf. "Ace in the Hole," the source story for the novel) and reports that their coach didn't consider Rabbit a "team player." (148) The constant talk about basketball annoys Ruth because "Every time I go out with this bastard we talk nothing but." (149) Rabbit also recalls post-game experiences with Mary Ann; in those days "He came to her as a winner and that was the feeling he missed since." (166) But those days are long since gone; now, Ruth tells him, "Maybe once you could play basketball but you can't do anything now . . ." (252) As far as she's concerned, both his basketball and his sexual skills are gone. All he can do now is run, run away.

STYLE: RUNNING METAPHOR

In the *Paris Review* interview, Updike told Charles Samuels that in *Of the Farm, The Centaur,* and *Rabbit, Run*, as well as in the short stories of *Pigeon Feathers*, the reader could find "a central image of flight or escape or loss, the way we flee from the past, a sense of guilt which I tried to express in the story, the triptych with the long title. 'The Blessed Man of Boston, My Grandmother's Thimble, and Fanning Island,' wherein the narrator becomes a Polynesian pushing off into a void." (93) When Rabbit starts out on his aborted flight to the south, he has intimations of becoming a sort of "Polynesian" dedicated to a long life of irresponsible pleasure. At the end of the novel, after much aimless running, he, too, pushes off into a void.

After the brief encounter with the boys playing ball, Rabbit begins to feel the urge to run again, and actually runs almost all the way to his home - and this is uphill, probably symbolic of the difficulty he will encounter in his subsequent attempts at running. (10) As part of her reception of Rabbit, Janice says, with some foreboding, "Don't run from me, Harry. I love you." (14) Rabbit associates running freely with youth, with his basketball glory. "I had nothing to teach you," Marty Tothero, his former coach, tells him. "I just let you run." (52) He goes to his apartment to get some fresh clothes, raps on the door, "braced to run." (83) He has run away from Janice, but he will also run away from Ruth. She tries to dissuade him from going to the hospital to see Janice; he is determined to go, and threatens not to come back to her, if she raises too much of an issue. She knows that he won't come back: "From the first night the wife would win they have the hooks." (161) Her only "hook" is sex. (157) The feeling of guilt over the baby's death sets him thinking again of running away. As he approaches Ruth's apartment, "F.X. Pelligrini" on the apartment door next to Ruth's is a signal: he, too, must be a pilgrim off on a quest. But a doubtful pilgrim, without sanction by faith (the unlit church window); the reminders of his former sins, intended or committed (sunflower, south side). (all at 224) Ruth isn't there to greet him; and when he does find her at home after the funeral, rather than forgive or absolve him of the death of the baby, she refers to him as Eccles, "fellow saint," "Mr. Death himself," "a rat"; then, "You're not a rat, you don't stink, you're not enough to stink." (251)

The final run, indecisive, aimless, ragged. (244, 245) Where shall he run to? To Janice and Ruth, to Eccles and his mother, "the right way and the good way, the way to the delicatessen-gaudy with stacked fruit lit by a naked bulb"? (254) He had almost been persuaded by Eccles' sermon on Christ's confrontation with the *Devil in the Wilderness* (197), but that way is too hard for him. He chooses, instead, the other way down to where the city ends in a vacant field of cinders, a personal hell. (254) The choice had been between the way of life - the right, the good, and the natural appetite (the delicatessen) - and hell. He doesn't turn right (in either sense) because he is still captive of his old conviction that external reality must yield before his internal feelings. And so he runs-into a void. (255)

STYLE: SEXUALITY

The choice between goodness and faith as against internal feelings and natural appetite is a hard one for Rabbit to make, since he has failed, according to Kierkegaard, to let his heart be "educated by reality." He trusts his instincts, and seeks a more comfortable place in sexuality, but even that quest is frustrated by his desire for "the hole without the accompanying net." And that path can lead only to a void, a blankness, to death itself. To understand fully the importance that Updike attaches to sexuality in the development of his themes, one has but to see how many symbols, images, and **metaphors** are sexually oriented. "About sex in general, by all means let's have it in fiction, as detailed as needs be, but real, real in its social and psychological connections," Updike told Samuels. "Let's take coitus out of the closet and off the altar and put it on the continuum of human behavior." (*Paris Review*, 102-3)

If rabbits could talk the way they act, then they would probably employ the same explicit or metaphorical sexual terms Rabbit Angstrom uses. On the very first page of the novel, Rabbit sees the ball "rocketing off the crotch of the rim." (7) In thinking about those desirable (and rich) Du Pont girls, Rabbit (Updike) clothes his sexual thoughts in euphemistic, poetic language. (25) The Amish, a God-fearing people, are described as worshippers of manure, who overwork their animals and take their sex of their women in the very fields themselves. (28) (Reference has already been made to the basketball images on pages 30 and 35, with their strong sexual connotations.) Whether it is an error in **diction** or intentional, he sees each car in the grove with its "silent coupling," rather than "silent couple." (37) In reply to Rabbit's question about the girls Tothero has lined up for them, Tothero "utters three obscenities in a stream touching a woman in her three parts . . ." (43) Later on, Tothero boasts of the way in which he helped his players develop "the three tools we are given in life; the head, the body, and the heart." Ruth adds, "And the crotch." (54) Harrison, Rabbit remembers, "had been a notorious bedbug," a lecher. (56) Later, he forces Ruth to commit fellatio, because he thinks she has done the same for Harrison. (157) Rabbit quotes part of his Magipeel Kitchen Peeler spiel for Ruth: "A simple adjustment of the plastic turn screw, and you can grate carrots and sharpen your husband's pencils." (61) Before leaving the restaurant with Ruth, Rabbit begins to talk terms for their pending assignation. The conversation turns into a kind of "courtship dance," a prelude, verbal sexual foreplay, the deal finalized by the plate that had earlier held sesame cakes. Open sesame! (62) Rabbit translates the $15 fee they had agreed upon as "a dime a pound," since Ruth had already admitted to weighing 150 lbs. (63) Rabbit is deliberate in his sexual preliminaries, so different from all the other men Ruth has known. "I know all about your systems," she says. "One squirt and done." (66) Rabbit's "squirt" is long in coming, and is fully appreciated by Ruth. (73) After that first session with her, Rabbit returns briefly to his own apartment. His car is "A sheath for the knife of himself." (82) Lucy Eccles is a "sharp vanilla cookie," vanilla being etymologically related to vagina. (104) But her husband can hardly appreciate her; he takes his vanilla literally, in the form of an icecream soda, in the company of less dangerous teenagers. (144) Finally, in un-Portnoy, guarded terms, Rabbit masturbates. (193)

STYLE: RELIGIOUS REFERENCES

Jack Eccles, with a peculiar mixture of Episcopal pietism and updated social psychology, tries to explain, if not defend, Rabbit's actions. The boy's problem, he says, "wasn't so much a lack of feeling as an uncontrolled excess of it." (142) Fritz Kruppenbusch, the more fundamentalist Lutheran minister, explains Rabbit's misbehavior as the ultimate result of a loss of faith. "It's all in the Book-a thief with faith is worth all the Pharisees," he says, implying to some extent that Eccles himself has been a bit of a Pharisee. "There is nothing but Christ for us," Kruppenbusch concludes. "All the rest, all this decency and busyness, is nothing. It is Devil's work." (143)

Does Updike agree with Eccles or Kruppenbusch? By citing Pascal, we must assume that Updike wanted to emphasize the spiritual nature of Rabbit's quest. (96) It may be that only through the process of something similar to Kruppenbusch's traditional Christian concept of grace that visions of "upward space" and voices call to Rabbit but do not call to other men (Eccles does perceive a kind of "saintliness" in Rabbit); and to pursue those voices Rabbit must harden his heart and remain oblivious to outward circumstances. But Rabbit's Christian vision is immature, despite its awareness of the need for a disciplined life, because it remains fixedly at the level of personal feeling. Rabbit does not have the makings of another Saint Augustine.

Eccles, a "fair young man with his throat manacled in white," (86) would like to think of Rabbit as a saint-or at least a convert. Once, Rabbit sees Eccles get out of his car, "and his head across the top of the car looks like a head on a platter." (108) The head of John the Baptist or is this John (Jack) the Episcopalian? (Or is Eccles to be taken as Ecclesiastes, the Preacher?) At the hospital, Eccles offers Rabbit a cigarette, and the gesture becomes for Rabbit " a wafer of repentance," which, for the moment, Rabbit gladly accepts. (164)

But on the whole the spirituality is more suggestive than real. Rabbit and Janice are watching TV together. When the chief Mouseketeer invokes the name of God in preaching to his (mostly) childish flock, "Janice and Rabbit become unnaturally still; both are Christians. God's name makes them feel guilty." (12) The old man at the gas station, in giving Rabbit directions, suggests one route to Churchtown. "Where are you headed?" he asks, and for the first time Rabbit feels that he is doing something criminal. (26) Still another slight twinge of conscience registers when he hears a radio commercial for Lord's Grace Table Napkins and the gorgeous Last Supper Tablecloth. (30) Soon, he is standing before Tothero's mirror - "Youth before the mirror" - and imagines himself the missing Dalai Lama. (45)

Ruth is more casual about religion. Her only recollection of Sunday School is that she was told that God made everybody good at something, and that her hope was to become a good cook. (65) The entrance to her apartment building is under a facade of stained glass; across the street stands a gray limestone church; both ironic heralds of the great "spiritual" experience that will await them upstairs. (65) The church to Ruth affords a "dismal view" from outside her apartment window. (69) The same view for Rabbit, the following morning, is more reassuring. "Its childish brightness seems the one kind of comfort left to him." (74) Later that morning, he says a silent prayer for almost all of his family and friends, and decides to go to church because it is Palm Sunday. Ruth doubts his sincerity. If he does believe, what is he doing here, with her? (77) After church, he persuades her to take a walk with him up to the top of Mt. Judge (read Mt. Judgment). All around them are people leaving church carrying "wands of green." Rabbit and Ruth are not among the "redeemed."

As part of his struggle for Rabbit's soul, Eccles invites him to play golf with him the following Tuesday. The church calendar lists that day as Shrove Tuesday. (91) Throughout this Sunday, however, he has been "bothered by God: Ruth mocking, Eccles blinking-why did they teach you such things if no one believed them?" (96) His own superior intuition tells him, standing there at the top of the mountain (Sinai?) that "the true space in which we live is upward space." (96)

Rabbit is now concerned that his sinful behavior may result in the baby's being born a monster, and that Janice may also die. He doubts there is a God. (165) However, he will try once again to regain faith by going to Eccles' church on Easter Sunday. (195) Lucy Eccles, with a surprised look worthy of Ruth, exclaims, "You're the last person I ever expected to see here." (198) The sermon discusses Christ's forty days in the Wilderness and His conversation with the Devil. (197) Rabbit's "forty days in the Wilderness" is thus properly adumbrated. Lucy, moreover, as surprised as she may have been on seeing Rabbit in church, must have had second thoughts later on: if Christianity is "a very neurotic religion," (200) then why shouldn't its provide for neurotics like Rabbit? But after the death of the baby, however, she can't see Rabbit as a Christian. "Christian! If he's a Christian, thank God I'm not one. Christian. Kills his baby and that's what you call him." (222)

Updike has said that "I've never really understood theologies which would absolve God of earthquakes and typhoons, of children starving. A god who is not God the Creator is not very real to me." (Paris Review, 101) To Lucy Eccles, "Freud is like God," and Rabbit, whom she calls a "primitive father," makes that seem all the more true. (99) She, for her part, feels that Rabbit is beyond redemption, and she, for one, will not try to serve as an "agent of grace" in order to help him.

Other "agents of grace" appear throughout the novel, however, and we shall merely list them to show how they attempt to carry out God's will in their own mysterious way. The first is the old farmer at the gas station. (26, 27) Then, Tothero, in his fumbling, Polonius-like way. (39, 47) Even before Tothero and the old farmer, there is the Big Mouseketeer, so convincing because of the peculiar mystique attached to everything on the television screen. (12) Eccles is an obvious choice - "I said as long as your heart remained open for Grace," he says to Lucy. (101) And to others. (90, 112-13, 139-40, 142) So is Kruppenbusch. (143) And, finally, there is the radio commercial (32) and the many signs on the road (35, 36). But Rabbit looks to the church in vain; to the church window, which because of the poverty of the church or the late summer nights, or just carelessness (sic), is unlit, "a dark circle in a stone facade." (254) So Rabbit runs. Ah, runs. Runs.

RABBIT, RUN

CHARACTER ANALYSES

Harry "Rabbit" Angstrom

Eternal Adolescent

During his visit to Mrs. Springer, the subject of Harry comes up; Eccles tries to imagine what Harry looked like four years ago, when he married Janice: "tall, fair, famous in his school days, clever enough - a son of the morning." (127) But Harry was already twenty-two years old at the time, a Korean War veteran, and already burdened with the responsibilities of maturity and a bride already pregnant. "Maturity" says Kurt Vonnegut, "is a bitter disappointment." Harry was no longer "a son of the morning," but he wouldn't admit it.

On the way home from work, Harry stops off to play a little basketball with some youngsters. He finds Janice completely relaxed, Old Fashioned in hand, watching television - not at all tired like a conscientious housewife. That's not as bad as a full-grown man "playing like a twelve-year old," Janice retorts. (14) Harry goes out to pick up Nelson at his parent's house. When he arrives there, he looks in through the kitchen window and imagines seeing himself sitting in a high chair. But the little boy is Nelson, not Harry, "and a quick strange jealousy comes and passes." (21)

After his abortive flight south, he arrives at Tothero's place to rest up. When he awakens from his nap, Tothero tells him about the two women he has arranged for them to meet later on. Harry is shocked that his former mentor is a philanderer, but is assured that Tothero's partner is a mere acquaintance, a "ladylove perhaps." Tothero adds, "Harry, you're so innocent." (44) Harry dresses - "Youth before the mirror" (45) - and is then introduced to one of the members of the Sunshine Athletic Association as "my finest boy, a wonderful basketball player, Harry Angstrom, you probably remember his name from the papers, he twice set a county record, in 1950 and then he broke it in 1951, a wonderful accomplishment." (46) Harry is innocent, as innocent as Holden Caulfield, as he fights his way through all the phonies in his life to recapture his glorious youth, a paradise lost, but one that probably never really existed. "Unfallen Adam is an ape," Updike said. "A truly adjusted person is not a person at all - just an animal with clothes on or a statistic." (Paris Review, 101-2) Can he ever recapture the greatness that Tothero speaks of? "I was great. It's the fact," he tells Ruth. "I mean, I'm not much good for anything now, but I really was good at that." (64)

In Harry's case, the child is not only father of the man, but brother as well. Ruth comments on the jockey shorts he is wearing. "In those damned underclothes you do look kind of like a rabbit," and adds, "I thought only kids wore those elastic kind of pants." (71) On their walk together that first Sunday, Harry is reminded of his own childhood - the Sunday papers, the dinner, and then the whole family on a walk. (80) At their first meeting, Eccles tells Harry that Janice is still unaware that he has left her, that Pop Angstrom told her that Harry had probably been sidetracked. Janice thought, according to Eccles, that since Harry had been late getting home that Friday evening from the street game with the kids, he might have gone back to it. But Pop Angstrom couldn't find the game anywhere. (87) The "game," however, is everywhere, a floating basketball game that Harry will pursue for the rest of his life. "If you're telling me I'm not mature," Harry answers Eccles, "That's one thing I don't cry over since as far as I can make out it's the same thing as being dead." (90) Or "an animal with clothes on" - a rabbit? - "or a statistic."

Man Of Feeling

Rabbit generally knows what "feels right." On his trip to the south, he is told by the old farmer to decide first where he wants to go and then go. But that was just the point, whether on a trip or in life itself. If he had trusted to instinct, he could have been in South Carolina by the time he had met the old sage. And Eccles, despite his clerical and moral obligation to persuade Rabbit to decide, then go, was encouraging Rabbit to live on the level of feeling, and thus avoid the rigor of intellectual and moral realism. Nor does he care about how anybody else feels, including Janice. "I don't know what she feels," he tells Eccles. "I never have. All I know is what's inside me. That's all I have." (91) Eccles insists that Rabbit is both selfish and cowardly. "You don't care about right or wrong; you worship nothing except your own worst instincts." (112) Rabbit doesn't deny that; he prefers it that way - to live in his skin (a baby bunting?) and not give a damn about the consequences of anything to anybody else. (125) "Goodness lies inside, there is nothing outside." (254)

Fastidious Harry

Pop Angstrom is surprised that Harry has abandoned Janice for another woman. He recalls how neat a boy Harry was, not sloppy like the other boys. In fact, Harry could have come into the print shop with his father, but "He didn't want to get dirty." (136) Now, before the "mess," Harry remarks how "he's the only person around here who cares about neatness." (16) Janice is so sloppy, so disorganized, so incompetent; and the apartment reflects her incompetence. Rabbit gave up smoking in order to feel cleaner inside. (24) He wouldn't live in Philadelphia, the dirtiest city in the world, unwilling to drink poisoned water. (25) Alcohol and cards suggest to him the greatest of sins, the sin of bad breath. (18) His rumpled trousers on the floor bother him. (44) The greasecoated pan in the sink bothers him, the remaining scraps of food adhering to the pan resist his hurried attempt to dislodge them. (84) With Janice at the hospital, Harry and Nelson take over the apartment. "Rabbit has a gift for housekeeping ..." (182)

Eccles begins to suspect the paradox in this preoccupation with the physically fastidious by a man who is hardly morally fastidious. "Do clean clothes mean so much to you?" Eccles asks him. "Why cling to that decency if trampling on the others is so easy?" (89) Nonetheless, Eccles feels sure that Harry will return to Janice because "He's fastidious." (131) And only Harry, the "fastidious" Christian, notes that the baby was never baptized. (242) "virtue is powerless . . . Virtue intervenes when power is gone." (Kazin)

Idealist

Fastidiousness, if carried to an extreme, may become idealism- or an obsession. In Harry's case, it's idealism. He likes Chinese food because it's so difficult to find the "disgusting proofs of slain animals." (55) When he played basketball, he never fouled. "That's right," says Tothero, "You never fouled. Harry was always the idealist." (56) Margaret has her doubts about that. "You're just a big clean-living kid, aren't you, you," she says, sarcastically, and Harry immediately hates her. (57) Harry's "disgust" with animal food is not based on a philosophy of vegetarianism (although rabbits are herbivorous), nor does his objection to Ruth's using a contraceptive device indicate where he stands on the subject of birth control. "If you're going to put a lot of gadgets in this," he says, "give me the fifteen back." (67) Spoken like a true hater of phoniness! Even when they are in bed together, he is still the purist. She must remove the ring from her finger, (70) wash the crusty makeup from her face (he does the washing), and he even dabs his own a bit. (71) Women, to Harry, are a different race. "In all the green world nothing feels as good as a woman's good nature." (79) The true thoughts of a true idealist!

Puritan

Purist or puritan? The difference is sometimes awfully blurred. Why does everybody who's telling you how to behave have whisky on their breath?, Harry asks. (28) Everybody? On his first trip, the thought of the pleasures awaiting him down south buoy him up. Then why does a lovers' lane that he inadvertently drives into become a "road of horror"? (33) He objects to Ruth's using the relatively tame obscenity, "stop screwing around," she a prostitute, he her "John" for the night. (69) Has he always been that puritanical? Pop Angstrom says it's only since he came back from the Army that he's changed. Now he's more interested in "chasing ass" than in working in the print shop. "Chasing ass" won't get his fingernails dirty. (137) After their night out with Margaret and Ronnie Harrison, Rabbit wants to know whether

Ruth will do "everything to me that you did to him?" He means fellatio, but he's "too fastidious to mouth the words." (156) In this "ritual," Rabbit fancies himself, if not a puritan, then at the least a priest bestowing grace on a communicant. Power in virtue!

Mystic

Fastidiousness can lead to idealism, idealism to puritanism, and puritanism-perhaps even to sainthood. (Was this the route St. Augustine and all the other great sinners took to arrive at a state of Grace?) Eccles had begun to put strange thoughts into Rabbit's simple mind. Rabbit has run away, but he's no fugitive, merely a vagrant, and all vagrants "think they're on a quest. At least at first," Eccles tells him. (107) Harry mentions Jesus, a well-known "vagrant," and Eccles recalls that He did say that "saints shouldn't marry." (107) The thought appeals to Harry. After all, there was something about John the Baptist in Eccles' appearance when one saw his head over the top of the car. (108) Moreover, Ruth said that Rabbit was loved by everybody, although she couldn't understand why. "I'm a mystic," Rabbit explains. "I give people faith." (121) Eccles had told him that, perhaps in jest, but Rabbit was beginning to believe it. Rabbit at first believed that he was acting evilly, but with Eccles' encouragement he now has the idea that he's "Jesus Christ out to have the world just by doing whatever comes into his head." (125) To Lucy Eccles he confesses to having intimations of a "new" Harry, a "straight road ahead of me; before that it was like I was in the bushes and it didn't matter which way I went." (175) Lucy, unlike Jack Eccles, is not ready to be taken in by the "new" Rabbit. But Mrs. Smith did believe that he had a rare gift, the gift of life. (187) Of such stuff are saints made. How desperately do we need saints!

Saint

Janice was the first to notice Harry's growing inclination to "sainthood" when he gave up smoking and drinking. (12) Other critics outside the immediate family have observed in Rabbit a "spirit challenging all adjustments to bourgeois society that bind the self to external standards at variance with the integrity of its inward vision." (Hamilton) Rabbit has also been called an absurd hero, "and because of the highly spiritual devotion of this gesture against the world, he becomes a saint, although a saint of a very special nature." (Balliett)

Janice (and Ruth and Lucy, too) should be numbered among the disbelievers in Rabbit's incipient sainthood. Tothero, however, is ready to believe in Rabbit because "he has not abused his body." (39) Not yet; self-mortification may yet set in. Eccles believes that Rabbit's sainthood may have been impaired by marriage. (107) Ruth fails to realize that the "unnatural" sexual act that Rabbit is asking her to perform is actually one of Rabbit's first attempts to forgive a great sinner-Jesus Christ to Mary Magdalene. (157) Rabbit's own renunciation of sex may follow, if we believe that he was turning down a genuine tender by Lucy to sleep with him. (201) Janice won't agree that the renunciation is sincere. (207) Nor does Ruth, albeit she does call him "fellow saint" of Eccles. (251) Who ever heard of a celibate rabbit? Only Tothero, who wanted to believe in Rabbit so much, is shocked at the outcome of Rabbit's noble "quest." "I don't believe that my greatest boy would grow into such a monster." (40)

Domestic

Rabbit, Run is a morality novel written about a period before Women's Lib in which many social critics were beginning to document an increasing disbelief in marriage as the foundation of everything. Soon after, Updike would question "marriage as a sacrament" even more vigorously in *Couples*. There is no doubt that Rabbit was trying to escape from the "unfathomable insatiable domesticity" of the Eisenhower Fifties (Kazin), even as he was (if we are to believe Eccles) "by nature a domestic animal." (131) Allowing for an unintentional pun by Eccles on the words "domestic animal" (a rabbit is also a domestic animal), Ruth is probably right when she says of Rabbit that "You love being married to everybody," (252) and probably to all at the same time. He will not divorce Janice to marry her. She refers to their first night together as "our wedding night." (68) He makes love to her "as he would to his wife." (71) By the following morning "They have become domestic." (76) Rabbit goes out to buy some groceries, to get some fresh clothes from his own apartment-in short, to settle in with Number Two Wife.

Relationship with Janice

Harry's relationship with Janice began when they were both holding down postgraduation jobs at Kroll's Department Store. The relationship became more intimate when one of Janice's friends provided them with an apartment in which to spend the night. When Janice was two months pregnant, they were married. From 1956 to 1959, their marriage was a standard, insatiably domestic relationship. From the very beginning of his first "escape" from her, he feels guilty. (26) The guilt becomes "a big bubble" crowding his heart when he has to admit that he's still married, married to the "twin" of a dumb girl. Rabbit has to describe Janice to Ruth and the others at the Chinese restaurant. (60) He is annoyed and embarrassed, particularly by Margaret's remarks (53, 57); she's a "shadow on his happiness," mainly because she reminds him too much of Janice. But Ruth is not interested in Janice, and so the "bubble" of guilt leaves him. (61) In bed he makes love to Ruth "as he would to his wife." (71) The "bubble" will not go away. On top of Mt. Judge with Ruth, he wonders: "What is he doing here, standing on air? Why isn't he home?" (96) Lucy, however, reassures him (sarcastically?) that a night's sleep without dreams is "the effect of a clear conscience." (172) After the death of the baby, she reiterates her belief that the marriage between Janice and Rabbit was an impossible one, that Eccles should never have reconciled them. "The girl had adjusted," she maintains, "and something like this never would have happened." (222) Rabbit "could almost have taken Janice, just as she was, sloppy, a bad cook . . ." (235) Moreover, she was right, even that time when he tried to get next to her when she was in no condition for sex, and so pushed her over the edge into the drunken stupor in which she drowned the baby. (225) It's just that he felt closed in with her, and so had to run. (244)

Rabbit on the Run

Rabbit solves the mystery of the two perfect disks-lovely life has been eclipsed by lovely death. (235) But the greater mystery to him is not "Who am I?" but "Why am I me?" The chief Mouseketeer had urged him, months ago, to "Know Thyself," as if that would have helped. He knows himself, and because he does, he runs. The "Why" of his identity is a subject for psychologists, geneticists, and, perhaps, for endocrinologists, as well. As for the moralists, they can always be out-numbered by the literary exegetes. And outvoted, too.

Ruth

Harry is immediately attracted to Ruth. She is a big woman (weight: 150 lbs.), and her thighs "fill the front of her dress so that even standing up she has a lap." (49) She's nothing like "that little mutt," Janice and more appropriate for "a big bunny." She likes him immediately because he's bigger than she is, and because she recalls how disappointed she used to be 'the way these little women everybody thinks are so cute grab all the big men." (78) She is apparently possessed of a good nature, unsoured by the profession she took up after graduation from Brewer High. She laughs pleasantly (49), and, "with the irritable deftness of a cat" can disrobe for him. (70) To Harry she seems to be a "tender entire woman," an "incredible continent," (70) the very incarnation of an earth goddess or whore mother.

The morning after their "wedding night," Rabbit is excited over the "idea of making it while the churches are full . . ." (78) It's Palm Sunday, and he's found a woman who finds him lovable, irresistible, because he hasn't given up. "'Cause in your stupid way you're still fighting." She also likes his sexual skill, so unlike the crudeness she has experienced with her former "clients." He is flattered that she has given in so easily, and is therefore surprised when, symbolically, she balks him on the golf course. "She stubs fat she stubs the dirt torn open in a rough brown mouth dirt stubs fat: with the woods the 'she' is Ruth." (110) But she is no crude prostitute. Her extraordinary self-respect insists that Rabbit divorce Janice and marry her before she'll take him back again. When he demurs, she dismisses him as Mr. Death, something lower than a rat. "Get out. Honest to God, Rabbit, just looking at you makes me sick." (251) Her idea of making love is to try to get close to somebody; (155) his idea is to replay every one of the basketball games in which he had been the star, the man running free. Ruth may not be as fine-grained as Lucy

Eccles, but she knows the meaning of loyalty, devotion, self-respect.

Janice

Janice is terribly weak and psychologically immature. When she married Rabbit, he was twenty-four, she was a small-breasted little girl just two years out of high school. She was overwhelmed by Rabbit, by his reputation and style, eternally grateful to him for having chosen her over so many other girls-Mary Ann, Peggy Gring, et al. She was an easy conquest; the wedding took place when she was already two months pregnant.(13)

Now that she is pregnant again, she seems to have stopped being pretty. (10) When Tothero refers to "little mutts like Janice Springer," Rabbit takes no offense. (48) The best he can say in her behalf (to Eccles) is "Poor kid. She's such a mutt." (89) Little Janice, pregnant, poses a threat to him. On the golf course with Eccles, Janice is one of the irons, "light and thin, yet somehow treacherous in his hands . . ." (110) When he misses the shot and is jolted to his shoulders, he believes that it was Janice who struck him. "Oh, dumb, really dumb. Screw her. Just screw her." She's a dope, a moron, but she's a frustration, too. "Come on, sweet, he pleads with his wife, there's the hole, big as a bucket. Everything is all right." (111) But it isn't; she has rejected his sexual advances, and when he misses the four-foot putt, he knows the rejection is final.

Rabbit can now take or leave a pregnant Janice, especially since he has Ruth. His mother thinks that he was right to leave Janice. "That girl wanted Harry and got him with the only trick she knew," she tells her more sympathetic husband, "and now she's run out of tricks." (138) Strangely enough, Mrs. Springer is inclined to agree with Rabbit's mother. The second time he leaves Janice, Mrs. Springer says: "The first time I thought it was all his fault but I'm not so sure any more. Do you hear? I'm not so sure," she tells Janice. (218)

Janice probably agrees with her mother. The drowning of the baby is unquestionably an unfortunate accident. Still the thought arises that she unconsciously wanted to drown the baby because it represented the obstacle (her pregnancy-induced unattractiveness to Rabbit and her postpartum condition combined) between her and Rabbit. She couldn't hold him except through sex; being unable to accommodate him, she had to let him go. He never really returns to her (even in *Rabbit Redux*). Poor Janice; she couldn't even make Rabbit a decent breakfast. (235) Man lives not by bed alone-even Rabbit. Still, he did keep hoping (before he met Ruth, of course) that "tomorrow she'll be his girl again." (11)

Jack Eccles

Eccles is a bit of an ass - "The fair young man with his throat manacled in white" (86) - a Pharisee, an ultramod minister- Hell without the smell of brimstone. He is obviously not John the Baptist (108) but Jack the Preacher (Ecclesiastes) bent on "brainless gaiety" in the "pagan groves and green alleys" of the golf course. (109) Holiness is not for him - "We're trying to serve God, not be God" (112) - so he concentrates on the very old and the teenagers among his parishioners, those who see him without his "white manacle." (200) He doesn't care too much for the more sordid basics of existence, especially little children. He prefers to read Belloc to his own children because Belloc mocks children, and Lucy cannot agree with him on that point, especially when those stories give little Joyce bad dreams. (106, 102)

He is determined to save Rabbit's marriage - "marriage is a sacrament," even a bad marriage (223) - at all costs. The ultimate cost, as Lucy sees it, is the death of the baby. (222) And so, sensing Rabbit's "primitiveness," his love for "purity," he takes him away from the world of gadgets to nature itself-a job as gardener for Mrs. Smith. He likes to feel that he has much in common with Rabbit, or at least Rabbit says so - "He and I in some ways I guess are alike," he tells Lucy Eccles (199) - and she readily agrees with Rabbit. Both Lucy and Rabbit are right. When Eccles calls up Rabbit to tell him the news of the baby's death, he says, "A terrible thing has happened to us." (223) They are "fellow saints." (251) Lucy does not think that a baby-killer, be he Christian and/or saint, should be admitted into a church. "Any Christian," says Eccles, "is in my church." (222) Moreover, any Christian can be guilty of all the Rabbit-type sins and wrongdoings and can be both explained (142) and forgiven. But not by Eccles, because Harry has done nothing "to me to forgive. I'm equal with you in guilt." (234) By Christ, rather, and through having gone through tragic circumstances. "This tragedy, terrible as it is, has at last united you and Janice in a sacred way," Eccles explains, and through the preservation of the sacrament of marriage, forgiveness will be forthcoming. (234) Such watered-down theology was good enough for Eccles' grandfather, and is now good enough for Eccles. He likes the color and the rigor that go with it. (106)

Marty Tothero

Tothero is a dirty old man (by his own admission), full of physical and mental deficiencies. He is a drinker, a lecher, and a bit of a homosexual. (38, 41) Both he and his wife agree that he is a person "to be abhorred." (48) He is a "vile old bum fallen among princesses." (51) Women, he tells Rabbit, "are monkeys."

(48) They have hair on every part of their body (47), and his very first announcement to the awakening Harry is about their coming date with Ruth and Margaret, accompanied by "three obscenities in a stream touching a woman in her three parts." (43)

Still, like Polonius, his advice is on the side of the angels, and like Polonius, he is full of platitudes and old saws. "Do what the heart commands," he says, and "Come to grips" with life. (47) One should develop the "three tools we are given in life; the head, the body, and the heart." And he really believes that "A boy who has had his heart enlarged by an inspiring coach" can never become a failure-or a monster-in life's game. (54-55) And Harry believes-or would like to believe-him. Next to his mother, Harry says, Tothero had had the greatest influence on him. (18) Harry, even Ruth admitted, had never stopped fighting, achieving, as Tothero had said over and over again. Tothero actually believed that, more than anything else, athletics could help a boy succeed in this achievement-oriented society, no matter what the undesirable consequences. For Tothero - and Harry - had, albeit unconsciously, accepted a "moral anti-process" along with the achievement-oriented society" to produce a very close facsimile of the Nazi Blood-and-Soil plus degeneracy faith - or shall we say at this point in time, a very close facsimile of the Watergate ideology?

Rabbit innocently and honestly thanks Tothero for having helped to bring him and Janice together again. (178) After the tragedy, Tothero tells Rabbit that the advice he had received had been good advice -The Devil can cite Scripture - and that Rabbit should have heeded it. (232, 233) Poor, dirty old Tothero -to have been chosen as an instrument of Grace for his finest boy!

The Springers

If we were to carry the Trap **Metaphor** one step farther, we might think of the name (or word) Springers as synonymous with "trappers." The thought is more than suggested by Mrs. Angstrom, when she refuses to believe that Janice automatically ceased to be a "tart" as soon as she received a marriage license. (138) Janice Springer had "trapped" Harry Angstrom into marrying her by letting herself become pregnant. (It is of course interesting to ponder the juxtaposition of "tarts" and "tricks," especially in the context of a wife having been displaced by a prostitute. But Mrs. Angstrom, we feel sure, was unaware of the association of "tarts" with "tricks.")

Whatever the true story of Rabbit's first "entrapment," the fact remains that he never really got to like Mrs. Springer. To him, she was "a gypsy, a fat hag, and a miserable nickel-hugger." (16) He had never forgiven the Springers for having given him and Janice a miserable bed that sagged. (83) Nor for having turned Episcopalian when almost everybody else around them was Lutheran or Reformed. Social climbers, they were. (85) Rabbit also feared that sooner or later Janice would duplicate her mother's plumpness. (236) When Janice needs a black dress to wear to the funeral, Mrs. Springer offers one of her own. When it looks at if Janice may fit into it, Rabbit almost blows his top. (237) She looks "broad and sooty in her mother's fat dress," even with the helpful pins and hems. (240) Still, despite the mutual hatred they have for each other, she absolves Rabbit of most of the blame for his second flight from Janice. (218)

The Springers definitely are social climbers. When Jack Eccles, their minister, visits Mrs. Springer, he notices that the house is expensively, but not very tastefully or imaginatively, furnished; "each room seems to contain one more easy chair than necessary." (126) Not only have the Springers subscribed to every strategy of middle-class life, (126) but they have also adopted a purely secular solution to the problem of Janice abandoned by Harry. Since Mrs. Springer conceives of Rabbit's motives as entirely practical, she is more concerned with what people will say about Janice than about the girl herself. Moreover, in order to get Rabbit to come back, both she and her husband will have to give him a good reason to do so. Mr. Springer immediately offers Rabbit a job as a salesman on one of his used-car lots in an effort to keep him with Janice. By this quid pro quo they carefully disguise their hatred for their son-in-law with a mask of social propriety. The ploy fails, not because of illogic on their part but because Rabbit refuses to-or cannot compromise with the reality about him.

The Angstroms

Mrs. Angstrom, like Tothero, cannot believe that Rabbit would hurt ("foul," in Tothero's parlance) anybody. (75) When Eccles meets Rabbit for the first time, he tells Rabbit that Mrs. Angstrom believes it's all an illusion Janice and he (Eccles) have about Rabbit's desertion. "She says you're much too good a boy to do anything of the sort." (88) Even to Janice, for whom Mrs. Angstrom had as much love as Rabbit had for Mrs. Springer. She never liked Janice's eyes in particular. "They never met your face full-on" (134) And yes, she tells Eccles, Janice did trick Rabbit into marrying her.

But Harry will come back to Janice, even crawl back to her. "He will, too, poor boy. He's just like his father underneath," she tells Eccles. "All soft heart. I suppose that's why men rule the world. They're all heart." (135) Later, at the funeral, her only thought is of poor Harry, the soft-hearted one. "Hassy," she asks, using the pet name for Harry when he was a little boy, "what have they done to you?" (241) "They" are of course Janice and the other Springers. But Mr. Angstrom is neither so blindly partisan nor so naive. He does recall the young Harry, constantly practicing to be a basketball player, always neat, always dedicated to the task before him, always wanting to be best at anything he was doing. (136) It must have been the Army experience that turned Harry from a career of chasing honest dollars (the Protestant Ethic) to the chasing of women. Neither parent can explain why their "domestic animal" went amuck.

Nelson Angstrom

Nelson already has two strikes against him - the little Springer hands. (191) And for this, Harry will never forgive the Springers. Even though Nelson, at age two-and-one-half, "walks like a trooper," (16) he doesn't have the hands needed to be a star basketball player. Nor is he showing, even at that young age, the ability to lead, to aspire, all the time striving to realize his aspirations. "He's been made too much of and thinks the world owes him what he wants," Mrs. Springer tells Eccles. Save for the hands, he does seem to have the makings of another Rabbit Angstrom. He even bares his teeth, rabbit fashion, like his father. (132) Rabbit thinks of Nelson as a little saint (Mrs. Springer thinks "sissy" would be more like it), a little saint (170), but no Rabbit Angstrom - not with those little Springer hands.

Mim

Mim is a slender, white-braceleted arm stretching across the steaming Angstrom kitchen table. (22) Mim at nineteen uses too much makeup, especially green eyelid paint. Mim is a barbaric creature dolled up for a Friday night out on the town. Mim is remembered by Rabbit as a poor eater as a child. Her mother, with an astounding prescience (she still doesn't know the less proper meaning for the word "tart"), refers to her as "Tart," who can't eat properly. (75) But Rabbit senses the direction in which Mim will go when he sees her at the Castanet Bar. He can't quite refute Harrison's suggestion that Mim is already a tramp. (152) However, tart or no tart, Mrs. Angstrom is convinced that Mim will not take a beating in life. "You watch her," she tells Eccles. "She won't mary out of pity like poor Hassy and then have all the world jump on him for trying to get out." (135) Not Miriam; she, unlike Rabbit, will have the guts to be herself, and make the world pay for it. Mom is right, as *Rabbit Redux* will prove. Mim will be the "success" that Rabbit always wanted to be-as an adult.

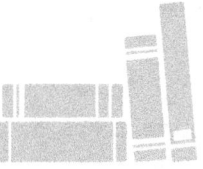

RABBIT, RUN

CRITICISM

MILTON CRANE

To Crane, the fact that Updike is talented and a master of the art of writing fiction is unquestionable. The question that does remain is, does the end product justify the application of such fine art to such a very grim story? The characters are creatures of instinct, floundering in a world beyond their comprehension. They are little more than puppets, and Updike in the end does not succeed in convincing us that these puppets are interesting in themselves, or "that their plight has implications that transcend their narrow world." (*Chicago Sunday Tribune* 11/13/60).

J. M. EDELSTEIN

Edelstein also feels that Updike's characters are not much more than symbols, poor symbols with hardly any of the characteristics of real persons, perhaps because he himself has failed to give us reasons enough to care for them. "It is also because of the emphatic selectivity which Updike has demonstrated in scattered sections of high poetic prose," Edelstein concludes, "that the book suffers and fails to cohere adequately into a novel." There is no question, however, this reviewer adds, that "at the envied age of 28, John Updike has become a figure to watch in American letters." (*New Republic* 11/21/60).

JUDITH SEREBNICK

"*Rabbit, Run* will be wanted by Updike admirers; but it is not a book to recommend without serious reservations." Some of the reservations: The ending is not meaningful enough; characters and situations often clash with the predominantly lyrical writing style; Updike may be a highly perceptive, sensitive observer-some of the minor characters are memorable, and the contemporary scene comes shockingly alive-but on the whole the novel fails to be provocative. (*Library Journal* 11/1/60).

TERRY SOUTHERN

The story of what is now the classic, lower-middle-class heel has been told many times before. *Rabbit, Run* covers the same field; it is a novel in which "the ingredients (including three ounces of earthy dialogue and a heaping big spoonful of compassion) are consciously added as though preparing a small stew, and the canisters from which they are drawn are the past works of a hundred hands." (*The Nation* 11/19/60).

TIME MAGAZINE

"If the power to shock may be taken as a yardstick of fiction, John Updike, 28, has written one of the year's most important novels." With the silent, sedate (sedated?) Eisenhower Years just coming to an end, the editors of *Time* still retained the capacity to be shocked. The reviewer found the story depressing and sordid, as well as sexually explicit. Still, the set pieces describing Rabbit's crackup, his confrontations with Janice, Ruth, Eccles, and other members of his family "show some of the surest writing in years," the reviewer concluded. (*Time* 11/7/60).

RICHARD GILMAN

Gilman took a more positive view of Updike's second novel. To him, *Rabbit, Run* was "a minor **epic** of the spirit." He also reassured his readers (and those of *Time*) that Updike was not suggesting that we should all abandon our spouses and responsibilities, and run. Updike, he maintained, was actually confronting us "with a vision of what persists beneath the adjustments we have made to necessity: the dream of freedom." The **theme**, he concluded, is a very old and honorable one in literature. (*Commonweal* 10/28/60).

WHITNEY BALLIETT

Balliett saw Updike in his second novel writing a new kind of prose through which to express his full-fledged misanthropy. If he displayed some degree of compassion in *The Poorhouse Fair*, in *Rabbit, Run* there is enough dissatisfaction with human fumbling to make up for the lack of sufficient reaction (by the author) to the pathetic characters in the first novel. Updike now shows no pity, nor does he show any humor either. There is, however, "a great deal of martinetlike understanding." As to Updike's explicit approach to sexual matters, Balliett concludes that Updike handles them "with precision, freshness, and grace." (*The New Yorker* 11/5/60).

GRANVILLE HICKS

For this reviewer, the qualities in Rabbit Angstrom that Updike chose to emphasize are most significant, and Updike's skill makes them all-too-real for us. Updike is compassionate, Hicks admits, but he also has so profound an awareness of human fallibility that he "treasures the goodness, slight as it is, that he finds in Rabbit." Hicks asserts that *Rabbit, Run* has now established Updike as one of our important young writers, a powerful novelist "with his own vision of the world." (*Saturday Review* 11/5/60).

WHAT THE CRITICS SAY

I cannot greatly care what critics say of my work; if it is good, it will come to the surface in a generation or two and float, and if not, it will sink, having in the meantime provided me with a living, the opportunities of leisure, and a craftsman's intimate satisfactions. (John Updike, *Paris Review* 100).

BALAKIAN AND SIMMONS ON "RABBIT"

If the reviews of *Rabbit, Run* were "mixed," the immediate critical excitement was no less equivocal. Some of the critics felt that a light-verse writer for *The New Yorker* would never intend any novel of his to be serious or significant. The critical reception of *The Poorhouse Fair* and *Rabbit, Run* was therefore, a kind of passing notice. The critics emphasized Updike's talent, his style, his poetic flourishes, his meticulous concern for the little details (and the little people) - always the word "little." The general consensus (at first) was that Updike "had bitten off less than he could chew"; that he was a "miniaturist" at best, a fainthearted (and faint-penned) writer at worst, a man whose reach never, but never, exceeded his grasp. The notion, insist Nona Balakian and Charles Simmons, is false, "since everyman's household, the scene of *Rabbit, Run*, may well be the true battlefield of the contemporary American **epic**..." (*The Creative Present* 215).

KAZIN ON UPDIKE THE GIFTED

Updike writes as if there is no greater pleasure, says Alfred Kazin. This pleasure and satisfaction with what he is doing comes out in his writing, so that the reader is always conscious of "Updike the Gifted, Updike the Stylist, Updike the Concerned Roguish Novelist." Updike is personal, without being subjective. His imagination is constantly concerned with the contradictions within every human display. The unmistakable presence of Updike in everything he writes, says Kazin, "finally seems not a hindrance but a trademark, youth's charming flourish of itself." It is interesting to note that Kazin is one of the few critics who don't hold Updike's youth against him, who don't suspect a precociousness that may become obnoxious even as it becomes enviable, and who don't detect a latent narcissism that can eventually become self-consuming and self-destructive. Kazin recognizes Updike's success in being an intellectual without becoming abstract. He respects Updike's ability to be a moralist without rejecting the mores. But above all he admires Updike's "cool," his poise. "If poise is a gift, Updike is a genius," he says. "If to be 'cool' is not just a social grace but awareness unlimited, Updike is the best of this cool world. All he lacks," he concludes, "is that capacity for making you identify, for summoning up affection in the reader ..." (*New York Review of Books* 4/19/73).

O'CONNOR ON UPDIKE'S DINGY, EVERYDAY WORLD

William Van O'Connor also notes that Updike is preoccupied with the dingier aspects of the life that little people lead. He also believes that Updike does this sort of thing much better than John O'Hara does. In *Rabbit, Run*, he observes, the reader finds no profound **themes** explored; instead, "there are acutely observed scenes, insights into character, and a sense of awe at the mystery of human sensibilities-all in an everyday world." Rabbit, for example, is hardly the reflective type. He feels, he sees, he touches, and his physical activities, as well as those of the other characters, are analyzed in great detail and with extraordinary sensitivity. (*Contemporary American Novelists* 211-12).

MAILER ON UPDIKE'S "LITERARY COMMERCIALS"

Like an older brother trying to tell his kid brother what's wrong with being a "beginner," Norman Mailer has some thoughts on why Johnny (Updike) can't write-or at least as well as he should be able to, if only he could forget about style and concentrate on the story and the characters therein. "He could become the best of our literary novelists," says Mailer, "if he could forget about style and go deeper into the literature of sex." (Since that statement was made, in 1964, Updike went on to write *Couples* and *Rabbit Redux*, both novels obviously belonging to "the literature of sex." One is curious about how Mailer would modify that statement today.)

Updike's style bothers Mailer (it's "atrocious - and smells like stale garlic"); for example, when the (conscious) style lets up, the characters are able to take over, and *Rabbit, Run* proceeds in "well-modulated spurts." "The trouble is," older brother

Mailer says, "that young John, like many a good writer before him, does not know exactly what to do when action lapses, and so he cultivates his private vice, he writes. And there are long over-fingered descriptions in exacerbated syntax," this selfsame paragon himself of the non-stop writer observes, "aimless crypts of four or five pages, huge inner exertion reminiscent of weight lifters, a stale sweet sweat clings to his phrases."

In the main, Mailer's criticism is reasonably favorable, and worth quoting at greater length:

The pity is that Updike has instincts for finding the heart of the conventional novel, that still-open no-man's land between the surface and the deep, the soft machinery of the world and the subterranean rigors of the dream ... A routine story of a man divided between a dull wife he cannot bear to live with, and a blowsy tough tender whore he cannot make it with, the merit of the book is not in the simplicity of its problem, but in the dread Updike manages to convey, despite the literary commercials in the style, of a young man who, is beginning to lose nothing less than his good American soul, and yet it is not quite his fault... It is a novel which could have been important,... but at the very end... the book drowns in slime. Updike does not know how to finish. Faced with the critical choice of picking one woman or another,... his character bolts over a literal hill and runs away. Maybe he'll be back tomorrow, maybe he'll never be back, but a decision was necessary. The book ends as minor, a pop-out,...

(*Contemporary American Novelists* 17-19)

Rabbit does come back-in *Rabbit Redux*. Perhaps Updike intended *Rabbit, Run* to be open-ended. Maybe for the benefit of Mailer and others, Updike should have added a simple Postcript: "To Be Continued." We put this question to Updike in a letter to him, and received the following reply: "The dictionary quote, giving the medical sense of redux, was my idea, and of course some such idea is intended - though maybe health should be spelled 'health?'... Though I can live with the medical meaning of redux, I chose it, as I think I've said, in line with Trollope's Phineas Redux - the simple sense, that is, of a character led back for another book." The reader should have no trouble relating *Rabbit, Run* and *Rabbit Redux*. "I wrote the second after rereading the first," Updike has written, "and they interlock and mirror in many ways..."

We shall attempt to illustrate this "interlocking" later on.

MIZENER ON ANGSTROM AS AMERICAN HERO

In an unrealistic work, such as a play by Shakespeare, Arthur Mizener observes, it is possible to tamper with the limits of the hero's probable self-awareness. Rabbit, being an unheroic, simpleminded hero in a very realistic situation, is incapable of such self-awareness; moreover, to suggest that he does have such a capability is to violate the **convention** to which the author is committed; or if he is not so committed, to "mix **genres** in an awkward and unpersuasive way." Rabbit joins the kids playing basketball and suddenly feels "like he's reaching down through years to touch this tautness" as he takes a shot. He cannot, however, translate his athlete's experience of excellence to a comprehension of why he cannot hit it off with his wife Janice. To expect him to be able to do so is "to pile onto a character a burden of transcendental perception greater than he can bear." The difficulty, Mizener continues, "is that this achieved sense of the promises of life and its constant redefinitions throughout the history of Western culture are the chief meaning of Rabbit's story, . . ." Updike, Mizener happily admits, successfully gets them in, by "mixing memory and desire, of showing the way tradition and the individual talent combine." In effect, Mizener is restating what Kazin has said about Updike, namely, that Updike is able to be a moralist without rejecting the mores. (*The Sense of Life in the Modern Novel* 255).

"MADDER MUSIC, STRONGER WINE"

"There's a 'yes-but' quality about my writing that evades entirely pleasing anybody," Updike has told Jane Howard. "It seems to me that critics get increasingly querulous and impatient for madder music and stronger wine, when what we need is a greater respect for reality. Too many people are studying maps and not enough are visiting places." ("Can a Nice Novelist Finish First?" *Life* 11/4/66).

INTRODUCTION TO RABBIT REDUX

FROM RABBIT, RUN TO RABBIT REDUX

"When I write, I aim in my mind not toward New York but toward a vague spot a little to the east of Kansas," Updike told Charles Samuels. (*Paris Review*, 89) Rabbit, the Angstroms, the Springers are all part of Middle America, the "silent majority," and in that respect may be said to be "normal," or "average." The spiritual or religious or theological escape from their "entrapment" offered by Updike is not always too convincing. But this is how we are, says Updike.

In *Rabbit Redux*, however, ten years later, Updike offers a more cogent, updated solution-social, cultural, political, and spiritual reform through the recognition and acceptance (and integration) of certain (not so silent) minority elements in our society-Jill, Skeeter, Charlie, Mim. Updike moves from the Silent Generation of the Fifties in a virtual quantum leap to the excitement and ferment of the Sixties. Since that fateful day in June, 1959, when Rabbit ran away, presumably forever, some very significant events occurred, up to the landing of the first American on the moon in 1969. To name just a few: the escalation and intensification of the Vietnam War; the Civil Rights Movement; the emergence of the Blacks as a militant force in our society; the demonstrations and riots in Watts, Detroit, and other cities; the peace protests; the takeover of Columbia University and other campuses; the Democratic National **Convention** of 1968; the Free Speech Movement at Berkeley in 1964; the surfacing of an extensive, palpable drug culture; and others.

Throughout all those ten years, Rabbit had been deactivated in a long Rip-Van-Winkle sleep. The war protesters, deserters, and draft-card burners, the longhairs, the aggressive Blacks, the total upheaval of the post-Eisenhower decade came to him as "agitated dream shadows on his TV set." Now, as the second book opens, Rabbit has given up sex, relatively speaking, as he has given up trying to recapture his erstwhile basketball skills. He says to Janice, "You know, ever since that happened to Becky, I haven't been that much for sex. It comes on, wanting it, and then something turns it off." (67) Janice has also noticed his loss of libido, and, rather than wait for him to reawake and take physical note of her (to "know her," as it were, in the biblical sense), has sought out a lover of her own. She has become a female rabbit, content to foray into strange "cabbage patches." Rabbit, for his part, will attempt one half-hearted sortie into another "cabbage patch" (Peggy Fosnacht), and will accept other "rabbits" - Charlie Stavros and Skeeter (a black "rabbit") - in his own patch. A few years back, he had met Ruth again, but all she had to say to him was, "Run along, Rabbit. You've had your day in the lettuce patch." (67)

RABBIT ON THE MOON

Rabbit, however, had had a vivid, exciting dream back in *Rabbit, Run* (234-5) of two perfect disks, one the sun, the other the moon. In that vision which, for the shortest moment, almost inspired him to go out and found a new religion, lovely life (the sun) was eclipsed by lovely death (the moon). Now, we know that the moon may be a lifeless body suggesting the deadness of Rabbit's own existence, but it may also symbolize something else. For example, in earliest, Pre-Christian times, the hare was one of many symbols of the moon, perhaps because the hare (unlike the rabbit) is born with its moonlike eyes open, and, according to folklore, is supposed never to blink. The hare was also, like the moon, thought to possess both male and female sexuality.

Moreover, since the moon **metaphor** is the controlling metaphor in *Rabbit Redux*, it was helpful to be told by Updike himself: "... I'm sorry we couldn't execute, on Redux, the jacket I had in mind, which was to superimpose on the little photo of the moon the rabbit in the moon you mention. The Japanese, among others, see him there, and indeed he's very distinct, if you look at a full moon in this hemisphere with your head tilted on your right shoulder . . ." (We Occidentals, of course, still insist that what we see in the moon is a man, and perhaps that is why we Americans may have gone to such great effort and expense to put a man there!) The reader may, therefore, look forward to a resurgence of Rabbit's sexuality in *Rabbit Redux*, thus permitting one to translate redux as "a return to health after 'disease.'" When Rabbit does come back (or is "led back"), he will attempt to join the "now" generation of athletes and astronauts. He will soon begin to imagine himself as an astronaut-or at least become one symbolically through revived sexual activity (sex symbolizing space travel in *Rabbit Redux*; in *Rabbit, Run*, it symbolized basketball, or at least replaced Rabbit's lost basketball skills - an interesting example of reverse or unusual symbolism).

TEN YEARS LATER

The transition from Rabbit I to Rabbit II is fairly traceable (and we shall discuss below some of the "bridges" Updike laid down).

"There is a lot of moon, of course, in *Rabbit, Run*," Updike wrote this correspondent, " - sun and moon (beginning of second section are a **theme**, and the jacket of that book [in the hardcover edition only] was meant to show the two circles, lunar and solar, of his dream late in the book." Also, the parallels between the two books - the death of an innocent girl in each book, more running, this time by Janice and Jill, rather than by Rabbit, etc.

BRIDGES

The new house that Harry ("years have passed since anyone has called him Rabbit") and Janice have occupied for three years is at Vista Crescent, the bar Harry and his father enter is called the Phoenix, Harry has been working with his father in the print shop for ten years, Harry's drink is now a Daiquiri (shades of that first Daiquiri he had when he first met Ruth) - all at page 14 in *Rabbit Redux*. "You've taken Janice for granted ever since - the time," Earl Angstrom tells Harry, alluding to the death of the baby ten years earlier. (16) Harry doesn't want Nelson riding on mini bikes, because he might get killed, as his other child did. (37) At the restaurant, the Penn Park couple paying their bill appear to Harry to be "laying a baby to rest." (52) The discussion on women and science leads Janice to remark that "Women don't dig science," (40) Harry to think of how sex became related to guilt, and that he therefore refrained from getting Janice pregnant again, although she did want another child. He was so sure that "Women and nature forget." (41) As it turns out, neither women (Janice) nor nature forget. When Nelson learns that Janice has left, presumably for the Poconos with her mother, his face "goes rapt, seems to listen, as when he was three and flight and death were rustling above him." (81) Finally, in a discussion with Skeeter, Harry innocently uses the expression "to throw the baby out with the bath," and then is suddenly reminded of "a tub of still water, a kind of dust on its dead surface." (216) The most significant of all the "bridges," however, is Nelson's premonition of a "replay" of the first tragedy, a premonition that the reader must keep constantly before himself. Nelson's "second sister" will also be "killed" by Harry, albeit indirectly.

Finally, a word should be put in for Janice Redux, for she, like Harry, also undergoes a "re-education." As *Rabbit Redux* opens, the reader learns that she, too, has been "led back," by Charlie, as much of an "exotic" as Jill, Skeeter, Mim, and some of the others in the Jimbo group. Harry approves; she, too, must have her chance to live (sex = life), and even to "run," as she does, after Harry refuses to be outraged by her admission of her relationship with Charlie. ". . . I was sorry you came back that time," she tells Harry. "You were a beautiful brainless guy and I've had to watch that guy die day by day." (71)

THEME AND STRUCTURE: OVERVIEW

Harry Angstrom returns to Janice in *Rabbit Redux*, illustrating Updike's contention that "Hell together is better than hell alone." Rabbit's return is inevitable (so is the sequel) because (a) marriage is a sacrament, (b) "Hell together, etc.," and (c) like the mechanical rabbit in a dog race, Harry keeps running around in the same orbit (!), never away, and always pursued by "dogs" (Cf. Janice as "mutt").

The book ends with Rabbit and Janice coming together once again with the cold, objective precision of a LEM docking with its command module following a mission. (Cf. the epigraph for the first section, a docking maneuver performed by two Soviet cosmonauts, to show the inevitability of the reconciliation.)

"O.K.?" (not "A.O.K.") is the very last word of the book, an approximation of space-astronaut talk, and is also, perhaps, our earthbound, now middle-aged author asking, "What did you expect? I do consider marriage a sacrament (see *Rabbit, Run*, 223), and sacraments do bring us to a state of grace. Moreover, I did give Rabbit another chance to achieve grace through Jill and Skeeter, through secular agencies, if you wish, and he muffed the chance." True; in this novel, Updike preaches a new gospel: "We must be nice to her, we must be nice to the poor, the weak, the black. Love is here to stay." (138)

But Rabbit, at 36, is middle-aged and middle-American. As the novel ends, he is "all passion spent." He missed his last chance for grace, for redemption, when he rejected Jill as child. (He always felt that his sexual relationship with Jill was incestuous.) He hates life (babies).

STRUCTURE OF THE NOVEL

It could just as well have be in the year 2001, rather than 1969, when Harry Angstrom started on his own personal "space odyssey." As the rocket is launched on that mid-July day in 1969, Harry (watching the event on TV) learns that Janice is unfaithful, that she is running around with Charlie Stavros, "an O.K. guy, for a leftwing mealy-mouthed wop." (62) But hitherto conservative Harry now finds that he can live with that situation; Janice, however, is amazed and deeply appalled, and runs away-to live with her lover.

In Part I of the novel - Pop/Mom/Moon - Harry is still "earthbound," watching the beginning of man's first successful landing on the moon. It is summer (*Rabbit, Run* ended in summer), and Harry has been in a rut these last ten years. The epigraph describes two Soviet cosmonauts in a docking operation. The sexual **connotation** is obvious, and we may expect a reawakening of Harry's sex life (the landing on the moon, for example). This "resurrection" will have to come, however, through very unusual sources -the black group at Jimbo's.

Part II of the novel - Jill-is concerned with Jill, the agent of Harry's "resurrection," but also possibly of his "redemption." The epigraph is a statement by Neil Armstrong, as he steps down on the moon on July 20, 1969. for some time, Harry will agree with Armstrong that it's "different but it's very pretty out here," as his "universe" begins to expand through his relationship with Jill, and then with Skeeter.

Part III of the novel - Skeeter-is prefaced by a most ambiguous epigraph, a background voice aboard the Russian space vehicle Soyuz 5 saying, "We've been raped, we've been raped!" From the contents of this section, the reader can adduce that Harry and Jill have been "raped" by Skeeter, or that Skeeter, in his lengthy review of Black American history, is emphasizing over and over again that the Blacks were "raped" by the whites. The latter is probably more plausible, especially if we analyze page 244, the key to the whole section. Therein we find the motivation for Skeeter's debasement and "castigation" of Jill. In re-enacting a section from the writings of Frederick Douglass, in which Skeeter assumes the role of the "white" slavemaster, he is punishing Jill ("black" Esther) for having consorted with Harry ("black" Edward).

Part IV of the novel-Mim-opens with an epigraph consisting of a quotation from the dialogue of astronauts Aldrin and Armstrong as they prepare to take off from the moon for home. The suggestion is there that both Harry and Janice will end their respective "flights into space" and come back together at home (wherever that may be, in 1969).

In addition to the "space talk" and the epigraphs, Updike provides several other time frames to help the reader orient himself timewise - the reference to the martyrdom of Mboya (22), the current movie, "2001 - A Space Odyssey" (22), Nelson described (23), Jill's reading matter, as opposed to Harry's "old world" (142), and Dos Passos-like "montages" (199,272).

Skeeter's "seminars" or "lectures" in Part III of the novel are significant for many reasons. First, they reflect the new awareness of the Blacks, in essence a time frame, too. Secondly, they represent a new ever-growing social awareness of the author, an answer, as it were, to those critics who have accused him of concentrating on the trivial. Thirdly, they change the whole tempo and tone of the novel; the action has been "frozen" as the novel becomes a tract for the times, rather than a story or piece of fiction. Skeeter's first lecture (203-208) is on the Civil War. The second (211-218) is on slavery. The third (227-232) is on Vietnam, and is more elaborately "staged" than the first two. For example, Skeeter looks up at the ceiling, as if it were a movie screen. Then again, the ceiling may be Heaven, and Skeeter may be interpreting Heaven. Or, the colored fragments may suggest the section in Shelley's Adonais; "Life, like a dome of many-colored glass, / Stains the white radiance of Eternity, / Until Death tramples it to fragments." And there is also the question, Why does the author, rather than Skeeter, narrate this lecture? The answer is that Updike can probably preach to the whites more easily than can Skeeter (228). The final lecture (243-248), in which a white is "raped," consists mostly of an excerpt from the writings of Frederick Douglass, which then becomes the model of Skeeter's "destruction of Jill."

Another new structural feature is Updike's use of interspaced (or interrupted) typesets (34, 164-169, 295-6). The purpose is manifold: to reflect Rabbit's disturbed state of mind, making it impossible to concentrate on the typesetting (the errors, incidentally, are standard for any qualified linotype operator); to provide an additional time frame; or to indicate Harry's expanded literacy and sophistication. (Note, for example, that the final typeset, the story of the suspected arson, is not interrupted.)

Once again, however, as in *Rabbit, Run*, we have another sexually-oriented "soliloquy" in the manner of Molly Bloom in James Joyce's *Ulysses*. This time, it is Janice musing. (55-57).

MAJOR THEMES

The reader can settle for three major **themes** in this novel: (1) the political **theme** of an immoral America, the "Benighted States"; (2) the spiritual **theme** of Rabbit's continuing quest for grace, this time available to him through Jill; (3) Rabbit's new role as a man of responsibility, a man ready to be reconciled with his wife.

Skeeter first speaks of the Benighted States at page 185. (The term was first used by John Dos Passos in a letter dated August 29, 1917, and may be found in *The Fourteenth Chronicle*.) Reference is also made to the "tiny elite" that the "rotten system" tries so hard to protect. (See also page 193) Harry still defends the Establishment, and even tries to put in a good word for President Nixon, but the "word" comes out this way: "Nixon, who's Nixon? He's just a typical flatfooted Chamber of Commerce type who lucked into the hot seat and is so dumb he thinks it's good luck. Let the poor bastard alone, he's trying to bore us to death so we won't commit suicide." (22) With the Benighted States just being themselves, even the Vietnam war is justifiable-or normal. (231) Harry has been worked on by Jill and Skeeter (and somewhat by Nelson) and now realizes that he must make a new commitment to civilization, even at the risk of losing some of that social and personal continuity he had fought to achieve earlier (in *Rabbit, Run*).

If five or six "agents of grace: could not save Rabbit (*Rabbit, Run*), how can one, small, fragile, mixed-up Jill save him now? "Man is a mechanism for turning things into spirit and turning into things," she tells him. (142-43) She also talks about ecstasy, about God, and the "messages" that man cannot see or hear because "our egos make us deaf. Our egos make us blind. Whatever we think about ourselves, it's like putting a piece of dirt in our eye." (143) But to Harry, Jill is something made of air or wind (or smoke), and is beyond his comprehension, at this point in his "rehabilitation" or development. "How sad, how strange. We make companions out of air and hurt them, so they will defy us, completing creation," comments Updike at the termination of a meaningful sexual interlude between Harry and Jill. (147) The "companion out of air" reciprocates by "blessing: her partner in the form of an unconventional sexual act later on. (157)

Back in the days of *Rabbit, Run*, the most serious charge made against Harry was that he was irresponsible. Now he is a very responsible man; Jill remarks that he is "Always worrying about who needs you." (128) Who needs him? Nelson, Jill, Skeeter, Peggy Fosnacht - and Janice. He responds to the first three, rarely to the fourth, and to Janice not at all. The new role must change Rabbit, and evidence soon piles up of this change. First, he takes in Jill, an eighteen-year-old runaway, and becomes both her lover and father. He is now responsible for a ménage of four - husband, wife, son, daughter. Then he takes in Skeeter, a Black on the run, and becomes Skeeter's "father" and rival for Jill's favors. He is now responsible for a ménage of six-husband, wife, son, son, daughter, brother. After death of Jill, he returns to his parent's home, regresses into adolescent fantasies worthy of a young Portnoy, and then agrees to take back his wife after she has surrendered her lover to his (the lover's) fears of a heart attack. In the end, a "more complex health and order is achieved." In the Fifties, non-hero Rabbit was running everywhichway, searching for spiritual answers. In the Sixties, he has returned to his wife, taken on a steady job and a mortgage on a suburban home, buttressed himself with a superpatriotic bigotry and a psychogenic antipathy toward sex, and settled down to enjoy all the cheap illusions he had fought against earlier. The brief but violent interlude with the Jimbo group, Jill, and Skeeter may or may not have affected him permanently. We may have to wait until Harry is forty-six (and a third Rabbit novel) to find the answer. If there is no third novel, then we must assume that Harry's little "space odyssey" has had no redeeming value, intellectual or spiritual, and that he is to be preferred just as he is-a typical middle American.

STYLE

Style: Language

In commenting on the changes in sexual deportment (Updike's term) that have occurred in American life since *Rabbit, Run* (published in 1959), Updike mentions Lady Chatterley's Lover and the Henry Miller backs, as well as all the other pornographic (or near-pornographic) books available in almost any retail store. "In *Rabbit, Run* what is demanded, in Couples is freely given," Updike concludes. (*Paris Review*, 102) In *Couples*, what is now almost acceptable, in *Rabbit Redux* is exceeded. The matter of content will be discussed in due time under Sexuality; at this time the reader's attention is being called to the very explicit language used in *Rabbit Redux*.

There is no doubt that Brewer (or middle America) has changed since 1959. The moviemakers have discovered that fact; so have the sociologists and the writers. (163) There is no doubt, however, that these behavioral and linguistic impulses have always been in Brewer. Note, for example, the language used by the two superpatriots who are trying to persuade Rabbit to get rid of Jill and Skeeter. (253) They use the more familiar obscenities as though to the language born; as though they have had ample occasion for expressing themselves uninhibitedly at American Legion gatherings, stage parties, and bar meetings. The difference is that in 1969 other elements in American society have decided to draw on their Anglo-Saxon heritage, too.

But Updike is no mere purveyor of a cheap "liberation through language." Nor does he intend to shock the reader and let it go at that. The language in *Rabbit Redux* (as in *Rabbit, Run*) is highly poetic, metaphorical, and suggestive in the best sense of that word. We shall examine once again the many symbols and images, the **metaphors** and motifs, that Updike employs so skillfully to embellish and enrich his language. In addition to these rhetorical devices, Updike now employs the wide range of tones and rhythms in Black speech. He has successfully captured the "melody" of Black speech, perhaps as no other contemporary white writer has. The added increment from this latter skill is the remarkable believability of Buchanan, Babe, and Skeeter. They are "visible" and Black.

Style: Symbols, Images, Motifs

All the many elements in the novel are presented from time to time in symbolic or figurative form. These several elements are then brought together in the controlling **metaphor** of space exploration (we shall treat this metaphor below), a kind of trip out into a void, and then back to earth, to life as it is. Updike has provided a kind of "bridge" in the simple phrase: "Putts. Fucks. Orbits." (26) From the golf image in *Rabbit, Run* to orbits in *Rabbit Redux*: "That's it!" Rabbit exclaims, as the golf ball takes off, freely, into space. (113, *Rabbit, Run*)

"I don't want him looking at mini-bikes," Harry tells Janice. The mini-bike suggests sex to Harry, and it was sex that led him away from Janice and so caused the death of his other child. Nelson must "Find the straight path and stick to it." (37) He must even resist the Gioconda, another brand-name mini-bike, perhaps a "happier" sex. (39), The mini-bike as sexual symbol is discussed fully under Sexuality below.

Janice's Falcon (read "peregrine," "pilgrim," "fugitive," or "runner") indicates that she is now the "runner," the roles having been reversed. The car is legally his (the flag decal shows that), but she uses it more than he does, to get to work, but also to get to her lover. (4, 83, 86)

There are many symbols indicating that the reconciliation between Janice and Harry has been a most tentative one. "He and Janice have not made love in the light for years." (68) Where Janice had planted bulbs in the garden during their first year in the new house, Harry finds nothing but weeds. (83) In addition to keeping Jill, he's also seeing Peggy Fosnacht, a measure of domestic "loyalty" in Brewer. Peggy has a job as a typist for Brewer Fealty. (222) He looks at their house in Penn Villas, "enough to see that it isn't Mt. Judge; that is, it is nowhere." (250) Home, after the fire, is Safe Haven Motel; it isn't Mt. Judge, it isn't even Penn Villas; it is nowhere. (346) He still longs for Texas; when he was stationed there during the Korean War, he was really free. (347) Now it is November; he is middle-aged, "all passion spent," in an "adjusted marriage," and all he wants to do is sleep. (349, 351)

He drinks Daiquiris now, a reminder of Ruth (those were the free days!), with whom he had had his first Daiquiri. When Peggy offers him that drink, he immediately associates her with Ruth. (99) Buchanan tries to dissuade him from drinking Daiquiris, "That is a lady's drink for salad luncheons," his Black co-worker tells him. (106) But he still drinks Daiquiris while he is discussing Janice with Charlie, her lover. He has a "second" one (the "first" was Ruth, the "second" one will be Jill, despite Charlie's advice to him to drop Jill). (162) When summer is over, however, he switches to a whiskey sour, a comedown from the Daiquiri; "summer" and youth (Jill, sex) are about over. (209) Peggy tries to delay the inevitable comedown. She mixes Daiquiris for the two of them, before they get into bed. (270) It is while Harry is engaged with Peggy that the house is burned down with Jill in it. Harry with Peggy that the house is burned down with Jill in it. Harry thus loses his second "daughter," and the mini-bike symbol proves to be an authentic omen. (Cf. 37)

Some of the motifs that were operative in *Rabbit, Run* are again evident in this novel. Orange as a symbol of passionate sex, for example: he awakens from a highly sexual dream about Charlie to a glass of orange juice served him by Janice. (69) There is a bright orange rooster on the birthday card he buys for Mom, and on the street outside, the inevitable Sunflower beer sign. (85) The sanitorium windows are "burning orange." (91) He sees a "very fat man with orange hair." (98) When he sets the name Oriole in type, he is reminded of his golden youth, sex, glory on the basketball court. (167) Peggy owns a golden puppy. (269) But the carpet in the motel is purple, and purple=blue (pure) + orange (violent, passionate) sex. (348)

Vanilla also comes back as a sexual symbol. (105, 157) So does the trap **metaphor**. (99, 162) The two are part of his earlier, "ordered universe," strange to say, the universe made up of ritualized games" (79): "The presence of any game reassures Rabbit. Where any game is being played a hedge exists against fury." (107) Even the Verity Press is reassuring, for there "We have a team here, we're in a highly competitive game, let's keep up our end, what do you say?" (192) The Crayola boxes remind him of the bleachers at the basketball game, "with every head a different color." (217)

Now Harry's "ordered universe," the kind of life he tried to recapture ten years ago, after the tragic death of the baby, is beginning to disintegrate before his very eyes. Even Brewer, 'the flowerpot-red city," the scene of his former Peter Rabbit escapade, is changing radically. The "local excavations" are beginning to turn up all sorts of "antiquities," as well as lots of "dirt." There is evidence that a trading post once existed there many years ago. (166) Now Brewer is a "trading post" where men and women can swap spouses. (163) Brewer suggests yeast, ferment, change, so unlike Mt. Judge and Penn Villas. And "that's why we live here instead of across the river over in Brewer," his ultra-conservative neighbors tell Rabbit, "where they're letting 'em run wild." (252) Everything moves faster nowadays, "except me," Rabbit says. (298)

Harry has tried to make some adjustment to the "new life." He has tried to get away from his superpatriotic neighbors (249), those voyeurs (251), anti-Semites (287), arsonists (290).

Maybe life is a massage. (85) Maybe one should let himself be maneuvered by those "magic fingers" of pleasure. (350) Even Janice has suggested that "there's no reason for two mature people to smother each other to death simply out of inertia. I'm searching for a valid identity," she says, "and I suggest you do the same." (98) So he accepts Buchanan's invitation to come down to Jimbo's. He's used to bars, "where they have everything. At home all I ever do is drink beer." (100) The bar represents a different kind of life, the Black singer Babe (110), Skeeter, Jill, Stingers, marijuana . . . He must stop being a "chicken liver," those who live in fear, without love, without heart. He must stop approaching Peggy timidly (don't count your chickens, etc.), and live, 1969 fashion. (241) He tells Mom that "Mt. Judge isn't zoned for high-rise," a sexual reference (erections) if ever there was one, but the **connotation** escapes Mom. It certainly doesn't escape Harry, who knows the true difference between life in Mt. Judge and life in Brewer.

| Style: Interlocking Images.

This device, as indicated earlier in the section on *Rabbit, Run*, has one image lead into another image into another image-all related, one echoing the other in a kind of reciprocal resonance. A simple example would be the image of Rabbit running to school, (165-6) which segues into Buchanan's comment that the money Rabbit is lending him will buy "a world of pencils"; (166) and finally on to mention of Dr. Kleist, the school principal, who owns a fine collection of prints. (167) A much more complicated example begins on page 130, where Jill is disappointed that she doesn't "turn on" Rabbit. The image moves to the next page, with the banner, "Clinic For Runaways Opened. Fathers Do Duty on Nights Off." Then to Jill's comment (same page) that Rabbit would probably find her mother a more satisfactory sexual partner. By this time, the reader should be suspecting that Rabbit's "inhibition" is a symptom of his dilemma: Is he father or lover to Jill? Is he about to commit incest? The rest of the images in the series serve to bear this out. On page 133, "cold moon" is mentioned, aborted sex. On page 141, Rabbit's discomfort while cohabiting with Jill reminds him of women who had placed razor blades in their vagina to thwart enemy soldiers. Rabbit is obviously feeling guilty about his relations with Jill. The series jumps to page 329, and here we have Rabbit reminiscing about his earliest thoughts on sex. As a boy it was a sort of space-flight. Now as he lies listening, Jill comes into him, leaves quickly, is merged with the moonlight, is referred to as daughter; he refers to himself as "father and lover," and also remembers her "daughterly blind grass-green." (330) From the green image to a slight reference to Rabbit's masturbating, which, like incest, is (or was) also forbidden.

Style: Moon Metaphor

The Apollo moon shot terminating with Neil Armstrong's landing on the moon is used as the integrating image of the book. (Since there are so many other non-astronaut references to the moon, we shall refer to the total device as a metaphor.) Rabbit learns of Janice's infidelity just as the rocket is launched. As Armstrong takes that "one step forward for mankind," Rabbit's terrestrial existence begins to disintegrate. The two middle sections-Jill, Skeeter-represent Rabbit's "free fall"; he is spinning around the dark side of the moon. Finally, Rabbit and Janice are home, in "space capsules," or like two exhausted rabbits in their hutch. All of 1969 America seems to be one great lunar wasteland, especially the suburban development (and especially the Angstrom house at Vista Crescent) where Rabbit and Janice live-it is nowhere, it is one of many craters on the moon. The urban blight that is so noticeable downtown-empty lots, abandoned or boarded-up stores, the garish shopping centers, the hamburger joints with their promise of a quarter-pound of bliss (plus a free American flag), the successive rocket launchings into outer space, the young people "spaced out" on drugs-all go to make up contemporary man's lunar landscape on earth. In short, everybody is free to "trip out" in his own fashion.

That is the general outline. The **metaphor** can now be "fleshed out" with more specific **allusions** to the text itself. We shall present them in chronological (with a few exceptions) sequence to show how the moon metaphor serves to integrate the whole novel. Brewer's technological contributions to the space program (see typeset) indicate that Rabbit's virtual ten-year suspension of sexual activity is now ready to end with the moon shot. (34) Janice lies "awake like the moon," (53) a symbol of sexuality, and also an image connected with the psychedelic section (52) referring to her disappointed sex with Rabbit. Charlie defines "space odyssey" his own, sexually-oriented way. (55) Charlie is Janice's most brilliant "planet." (58) On page 58, the astronauts are approaching the moon's gravitational pull; Harry is soon to become sexually adventurous again. "Apollo Eleven is in lunar orbit and the Eagle is being readied for its historic descent." (81) Harry is also getting ready. Is there any life on earth? This is an indirect reference to the moon, where there is real, i.e. sexual, life. (85, 86, 87) The Eagle lands, ironically on the Sea of Tranquillity. (88) Tranquillity for Harry? He thinks about that Texas moon back in 1953, and of his experiences in a whorehouse. He didn't pay to be a "two-timer" then, but he has been - and will be again -a "two-timer," with or without paying for the privilege. But astronauts (and Harry) are not completely free. The Command Module keeps orbiting the moon. (89) There are some controls over unrestricted sexuality - Houston and Ft. Hood, both checking on "two-timing." Man is now on the moon.

(92) The rabbit may now also be considered to be on the moon (Cf. Japanese myth in Introduction); Rabbit has decided to leave his "spacecraft," that "long empty box in the blackness of Penn Villas, slowly spinning in the void." In his "expanding universe," he is once again ready to make sexual contact, this time with Jill, (95) an event forecast in the very first epigraph, the docking maneuver.

The epigraph for Part II signals Rabbit's intention to leave the old, dead world of Pop, Mom and the conservative life, for the new, "expanding universe" of Jill (the moonchild), Skeeter, and Mim. Note the transition from Pop/Mom/Moon to Pop/Mom/Mim or Janice/Nelson/Mim. Jill offers Harry love; he is not so sure he wants love. The moon is cold and ugly. (152) Jill is a moonchild, he is an earthman (his mother has called him a "lump," earthbound); but they can still link up together. (175, 179) But Astronaut Rabbit will soon have to go back to his abandoned "space capsule" at Penn Villas. He and Jill (also Nelson and Skeeter) are out walking (her car is waiting to be towed away). There is a quarter-moon, "with one sick eye," scudding over the flying horse sign. (237) It may be Vista Crescent for Harry. Jill as moonchild (238) will soon be gone. When they return to the "bleak terrain of Penn Villas" in the rented car, the "odd car load" is like growths festering on the surface of the moon." (238) After the fire, with Jill gone, a half-moon hovers over Harry as he is approached by the watchman. (287) Harry's relationship with Jill as a father has ended. "The freshening sky above Mt. Judge is Becky, the child that dies, . . . " Janice awakes to see the moon, "a cold stone above Mt. Judge." (333) There is no sex in Mt. Judge, only in Brewer. Harry and Janice have finally come to a "docking" (Cf. epigraph, Part IV), and as they are still "adjusting in space," he can already feel themselves drifting "along sideways deeper into being married." (350) They are now locked into their own little capsule, the motel room, the burrow-two rabbits coming back from their trip to the moon.

Style: Rabbit Metaphor

It is possible that Updike may have intended *Rabbit Redux* as a kind of sophisticated nursery fable or parable for grown-ups. Rabbit is naughty, very naughty, and runs away into strange cabbage patches. Eventually, however, he is punished, chastened, and led back to his own cabbage patch. That, however, would be too much of an oversimplification. For one thing, the Rabbit **Metaphor** is not too prominently developed in this book. (There are a few references: 14, 349, 351, 301.) For another, the name Rabbit is less sparingly used (see origin of nickname, 14); Harry is more often preferred. Still another point: there is very little running (a rabbit characteristic, especially in *Rabbit, Run*) in this book on the part of Harry (Cf. 53, 152), more so on the part of Janice, and in the main instance, in which Harry, Nelson, Jill, and Skeeter may be presumed to be trying to "run," they are thwarted when the car is "seized up." (236) The rabbit image is operative, however, to some extent in the Basketball Metaphor.

Style: Basketball Metaphor

In *Rabbit, Run*, Rabbit was a forward or center (in basketball terminology), but always a "man in motion." In *Rabbit Redux*, he becomes a stationary center (in the manner of Wilt Chamberlain), a "high pick" (in basketball lingo) holding the ball, but ready to pass it off to others who may "shoot for the hole" or the basket. In both basketball and sex, he has yielded the option to others-Charlie with Janice, Skeeter with Jill, for example. Thus, Skeeter reminds him of the new type of basketball player, "big looping hungry blacks lifting and floating there a second while a pink palm long as your forearm launched the ball." (25) Stavros reminds him of the playmakers on a team, "guys, close-set, slow, and never rattled, . . ." (44) Stavros is dangerous as a playmaker who can outtalk, outreason, and outmaneuver Harry. He has "sneaked in for that lay-up and the game is in overtime." (163)

Rabbit would like Nelson to become a basketball player, too, but that cannot ever happen (those little Springer hands); not with all those clippings about Rabbit's former basketball exploits that Mon pasted into a scrapbook. Nelson becomes even more discouraged every time he reads about what "happened twenty years ago, light from a star." (25) And Rabbit was a star! Should he put up a basketball hoop on the garage? (31) That's how he learned to shoot many, many years ago. Life actually stopped for Rabbit once basketball stopped. (178) Occasionally, flashes of his former skill come back, as in a discussion with Jill, Skeeter, and Nelson. "Three on one: Rabbit is exhilarated. Faking and dodging." (200) When he wins a debating point from Skeeter, it's like "Having scored, you put your head down and run back up the floor; but with that feeling inside, of having made a mark that can't be rubbed out." (201) He explains our Vietnam policy to Skeeter in basketball terms, the one language that he considers himself complete master of. (310-11) But in the end, the ultimate **irony** is that running in life, like "travelling" in basketball, became an offense in the game of life, as well as in the game he had excelled in. (328)

THE BLACKS

"You're gone to be our big nigger tonight," Skeeter tells Harry, just as Harry is about to read aloud passages from *The Life and*

Times of Frederick Douglass. "As a white man, Chuck, you don't amount to much but niggerwise you groove" (243) Harry is inclined to believe this ever since Skeeter (mosquito) began to aim "stingers" at him in the Jimbo Friendly Lounge. With Skeeter a resident "instructor" in his home, Harry's whole concept of the Blacks is changing even more rapidly than before. He has come a long way since he complained that the bus "stinks of Negroes." (40) Now he is harboring a Black "fugitive from justice" in his very own, conservative home, so how can he ignore the Black Revolution that is taking place all around him? He knows about the Black riots in York from the newspapers and television reports. (58) He would like to stay with the white backlash, which is more his cup of tea (47, 49), but Skeeter (and Jill and Nelson) have been working on him, especially through those "seminars" that Skeeter has been conducting. It is doubtful if Harry can ever become a "White Negro" or "hipster" - Mailer's term - he would have an awfully long way to go - but Skeeter will try to re-educate him. Mailer, by the way, claims that when the bohemian and the juvenile delinquent came face-to-face with the Negro, the hipster was produced. In Harry's ménage-a-trois, we have the juvenile delinquent (Jill), the Negro (Skeeter) and the "bohemian" (Harry, pace for the sake of illustration). In the wedding of the white and the Black, "it was the Negro who brought the cultural dowry," says Mailer. ("The White Negro," in *Advertisements for Myself*, 306). By his very presence, and more systematically, through the "seminars," Skeeter proceeds to introduce Harry to the Black cultural dowry.

How far does Harry have to go before he can qualify for skeeter's honorary title of White Negro? Before Skeeter's arrival at Vista Crescent, Harry didn't argue when his father blamed the Blacks for the many thefts in their area and elsewhere. (148) Nor did Harry enter a demurrer when his father assured him that the American Blacks "are the lowest of the low." (149)

Harry himself complained that "these black kids on buses are pushy as hell"; (219) Nelson complained about their "fat lips." (84) Harry is being let out of his job, Buchanan (one of the two Black workers at the Verity Press) is to be kept on so that the Equal Opportunity forces in the city are not antagonized. "I'd just as soon have a moron with mittens on as long he was white-," Pajasek tells Harry (297), but Harry makes no attempt to defend Buchanan as a man, a co-worker, and his sponsor (he did introduce Harry to Babe, Skeeter, and to Jill, after all). Moreover, if Harry is "tired of white meat" (Jill) and would like a "drumstick" (Black woman), Buchanan is ready to fix him up with Babe. (166)

The texts or "holy books" that Skeeter uses in trying to convert Harry to a "White Negro" are interesting in that they can be found today in the bibliography for any Black Studies course in the United States. They include *The Selected Writings of W.E.B. DuBois, The Wretched of the Earth, Soul on Ice*, and *The Life and Times of Frederick Douglass*. Supplementary materials include the Lone Rander-Tonto parable (212, 30-31) and the preliminary indoctrination sessions at Jimbo's. All this intensive teaching by Skeeter has an unmistakable effect on Harry (too subtle, perhaps, to be noticed within the limited scope of the novel), and also reveals that Skeeter, far from being a Black Power advocate (he has no love for Huey Newton and Stokely Carmichael, or any of the other "Establishment Niggers"), is actually an apocalyptic character who fancies himself a Black Jesus Christ. Skeeter's concept of black-white equality is Vietnam, "the only place in Uncle Sam's world where black-white doesn't matter." (228) There white boys were willing to die for him, and the Army treated the Blacks well because a "black body can stop a bullet as well as any other, they put us right up there, and don't think we're not grateful, we are indeed, we hustle to stop those bullets, we're so happy to die alongside Whitey." (228-9) The enigma of Skeeter, therefore, may more properly be discussed under the heading of Religious Influences.

RELIGIOUS INFLUENCES

"In their frailty things keep faith," Updike says, and this may well serve as the text for any spiritual examination of the novel. (325) The religious overtones in the novel are too numerous to examine in full, but emphasis should be placed on the fact that the whole Skeeter section may be construed as a Christian parable, an apocalyptic, new Book of Revelation. The "gloss" (a quotation from Ecclesiastes) on Babe's singing is definitely religious. (115) Finally, Jill's delicately spun image of God is still another manifestation of the spiritual (the case has already been made for the moral) tone of the novel.

As Babe "reads" Harry's knuckles at Jimbo's, Skeeter is quick to point out that Harry and all the other Charlies (whites) are so mean because they have too much religion. It is their God who tells them that it is both moral and God-serving to have intercourse with every Black girl who comes their way. (108) This same God, Skeeter tells Harry, is "a pansy". Your white God's queerer than the Queen of Spades . . . Another thing. Ain't no Jesus. He was a faggot crook, right? . . ." (187) Harry should also keep in mind that Vietnam has more than military importance for the world. "It is the local hole," Skeeter maintains. "It is where the world is redoing itself . . . It is where God is pushing through . . . Chaos is His holy face." (230) Nelson is frightened by this description of God; he would prefer God to remain as He is. Skeeter answers that to accept an unchanging God is to be a slave, like his father, who is average and ordinary." Harry refuses to buy this "revelation" of Skeeter's. Vietnam is just a dirty, necessary war, and Skeeter can't make "something religious out of it just because you happened to be there." (231)

So much for Skeeter's effort to re-educate Harry spiritually. (More examples will be given in the analysis of Skeeter's character.) Now for Jill's efforts at doing the same for Harry. God has changed for her since she was in junior high school. Now He is something like the inside of a very big lily. (132) She discusses God and beauty with Nelson, too. God and religion have inspired man to produce many beautiful things. "Man," she says, "is a mechanism for turning things into spirit and turning spirit into things." (142-3) Moreover, man does not influence God, she tells Harry. "He does everything by the way. Not because it's what He has to do." Finally, she says, "God is in the tiger as well as in the lamb. (146) This is less than reassuring to Harry, who identifies the tiger with Janice (Charlie called her that first) and the lamb with Jill. But what about the rabbit? "In their frailty things keep faith." God is for Harry, too.

SEXUALITY

It may seem irreverent to consider sexuality in such close proximity with the religious and the spiritual, but it is that very dualism that is at the heart of this book. "In the microcosm of the individual consciousness," Updike has said, "sexual events are huge but not all-eclipsing; let's try to give them their size." (*Paris Review*, 103) Since 1959, language has been liberated, especially in relation to the body parts, body functions, and sex. Harry has libidinous thoughts about a Black bride, and muses on Black sexuality in very explicit terms. (25) Janice has learned to use many of the more common four-letter words without any degree of self-consciousness. (38) Nor does she think language should be inhibited in front of Nelson. (41) Harry, for his part, sees sexuality in everything, including a cigar. (59) In questioning Janice about her relationship with Charlie, he comes right to the point, language-wise. (61) And Updike, for his part, puts some of the choicest phrases of what used to be called "gutter language" or "locker-room language" into Skeeter's description of God and Jesus Christ. (187)

Some of the sexual images are fairly obvious. Harry dreams of taking a motor trip with Charlie Stavros. When their route takes them to a metropolis called The Rise (and marked with a bull's eye), he suddenly awakes, with a headache and an erection. The erection may be traced back to his earlier sexual encounters with Janice (also the headache), or to his anxiety over Janice's affair with Charlie, or to the symbols themselves in the dream. Freud would have had a lot of fun with that dream. A simpler sexual symbol is Harry's thumb, being discussed not as qua thumb but as penis. (108, 109) Harry's apparent initial rejection of Jill leads Buchanan to ask him if he is going to go off "half-cocked." (113) The "fucking mini-bike" (is the adjective operative or pejorative?) is a sexual symbol, even without the accompanying adjective. "Mom," Billy tells his mother, "the fucking thing broke down again." (103) The reference may first be to the interrupted sexual encounter between Peggy and Harry. Then, when Nelson is blamed for the collapse of the mini-bike, Harry says, "You baby, I didn't say that exactly." In effect, Harry is saying that it was not Nelson's fault that the sexual relationship between Harry and Janice failed, but the baby Rebecca's. Much later, Peggy speaks of her probable reconciliation with her husband Ollie, who also brought a gift for Billy. "Another mini-bike," Harry asks, implying that the reconciliation may be a "complete" one. Peggy tells him that this time the gift is a puppy. In other words, there is still a chance for Harry with Peggy. (222).

Harry has always had ambivalent feelings about Jill (discussed earlier), and on occasion refers to her as "cheap vanilla" or cheaply held sex. However, after he has slapped and twisted her arms (152), he repents his cruelty. The "act of repentance" takes the form of cunnilingus, and Jill feels that she has triumphed over her enemy. (It is interesting to note that in *Rabbit, Run*, Harry has Ruth perform fellatio on him, Both incidents, by coincidence, occur at page 157 in each book.) Again, on page 260, Jill re-enacts with Skeeter the act of fellatio that Ruth had performed on Harry in *Rabbit, Run*. True, there is poetry, there is euphemism, but the raw fact of sexuality comes through. Since *Rabbit, Run*, Updike has moved a long way toward explicit language, and *Rabbit Redux* provides many examples of this liberated approach.

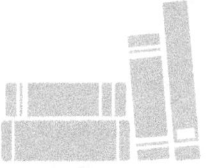

RABBIT REDUX

CHARACTER ANALYSES

Harry Angstrom

Old Athletes Never Die

Harry, watching a baseball game with his son and father-in-law, envies the players because they seem to be experts or specialists like any other highly talented people, "not men playing a game because all men are boys time is trying to outsmart." (79) As long as Harry retained his basketball skills, he remained a boy, impervious to the threat of time. Now, those skills long departed, he is still trying to outsmart time.

Janice is aware of Harry's losing fight. She sees her "flying athlete grounded, cuckolded." (39) Pop knows that Harry is now a big boy, a responsible citizen; Harry knows it, too, but he is uncomfortable in the role. (59) Ruth recognized it about three years ago (perhaps earlier), but she couldn't convince Harry that the Peter Rabbit bit was now much too ridiculous for him. (67) His inability to react to Janice sexually seems to confirm this. (65) In fact, she feels sorry that he had returned that last time (after the baby's death) because she must now watch a "beautiful brainless guy" slowly die "day by day." (71) Buchanan also agrees with Janice. (97) He introduces Harry to the others at Jimbo's as a great basketball player, but that was in the Brewer "in his day." (107) Tothero always attested to Harry's greatness, (113) and now Jill is expected to accept him as "Harry the Rabbit Angstrom." (115)

But he's old, fat and finicky now, and when he tries to take a shot at the basket with Nelson's soccer ball, he misses. "The touch is gone," he confesses. "When you get old, the brain sends out the order and the body looks the other way." (224) He's an old athlete with a beer gut. (212) "You gotta jump and shoot, jump and shoot, right?" Skeeter tells him, but he can't, not with a "white man's lead gut." (239) From here on in, Harry's got to learn to be a loser because God loves losers, and losers, like the meek, shall inherit the earth. (268) Mim also sees the potential loser in him; he's gotten soft, "like slugs under fallen leaves," she tells him (313) Right; he no longer believes in force, (318) he won't even fight a little, (193) and a man without force is "without the essential dignity of humanity." (247)

Retreat to Adolescence

Back in his parents' house after the fire, Harry finds some compensation for his loser's role in reversion to adolescent fantasies: boyish foods from his childhood, (304) the strippers in his favorite comic strip, (323) a random shot at the basketball hoop on his father's garage, (325) peanut-butter sandwiches and masturbation, (327) more masturbation, because as he gets older "real people aren't exciting enough," (328) and an imagined version of Stavros and Mim locked in sexual intercourse. (329) "It was an ice cream world he made his mark in," he muses (340) and sex then was so much more like a flight into outer space. (329)

Conservative-of What?

He's a loser who feels personally and sexually threatened, and so he vigorously defends the Vietnam War, traditions, the Establishment, outdated morality, and the phoniness of superpatriotic platitudes. He puts a flag decal on the rear window of his old Falcon over the objections of Janice that it's both corny and fascist. (21) She says it's a sign of how uptight he's gotten in his old age, (38) that people are "more sophisticated now than when you were a boy." (41) The flag decal hits Charlie the same way. (46) Harry won't argue politics with Charlie because it's one of his "Goddam precious American rights" not to think about it. (47) He prefers to live an old-fashioned life, (54) something that won't appeal to Charlie, an "O.K. guy, for a left-wing mealy-mouthed wop." (62) Harry is satisfied to be a God-fearing patriot (106), a square, an innocent, a Huck Finn to Buchanan's Jim, (111) satisfied to go back to an America that was "the wisest hick town within a boat ride of Europe and Broadway..." (114) Babe's music reminds him of those old days of "circus tents and fireworks and farmers' wagons and an empty sandy river running so slow the sole motion is catfish sleeping beneath the golden skin." At Jimbo's he is Huck Finn floating down the Mississippi on a raft with Jim.

Harry senses that he must be out of step with everybody else, lobotomized, as it were, so that he can't say "Black" instead of "Negro," or hate the Vietnam War. (198) He's tried to meet progress halfway-a beer and a marijuana joint, a paradox, but an attempt to compromise. (257) So what if Janice considers him a conservative? (254) Sure, but the kind of conservative that voted for Hubert Humphrey, just as his father did. (280) So he'll just keep that flag decal on his car window; it's a bit faded, but it still looks aggressive-like him. (340) The answer, says Harry, is to go back to school again, to reconfirm the order as it is. (171)

The "Saint" That Was

Fastidious Harry really hates sex. (57) When Janice makes a sexual overture, "he brushes her away with an athlete's old instinct to protect that spot." (32) In all these ten years since the death of the baby, he has consciously avoided her, equating sex with death, trying not to let her have another baby to replace the lost one. (33) Besides, he thinks-after some very active coition with Janice that he did agree to after all-sex has an aging effect on men. Look how boyish priests remain, how few gray hairs spinsters have in their head, even up to age fifty. "We others, the demon rots us out." (69) Now Janice is carrying on with Charlie Stavros; he should care, but he doesn't. If Charlie can make Janice happy (at least much more often than he can, or wants to), she can keep him. (70) Harry welcomes the chance to be a martyr, the wronged one, the abandoned one, for a change.

Harry's prudishness carries over into his attitude toward pornography; it always leads to sex, he believes. He must check on Nelson to see that the boy isn't buying dirty pictures. (99) Even the men at the shop go in for porno and girlie pictures. (100) It's the fault of the Supreme Court that all the bars have been let down. Then there's Peggy, making very suggestive gestures toward him. Should he or should he not resist the temptation to take her? He will-at least for the time being. (103, 104) He enjoys the sensation of being temporarily virtuous.

Jill, however, is something else. She's no Peggy, no box of gumdrops. She's more direct, knows all the latest sexual maneuvers, is willing to "service" a man any which way. He holds off for the time being. (130) Something in his subconscious seems to be telling him that it isn't quite right to have sex with this young thing. (131) He chides her for having run away from her family (the sinner turned preacher), and she appreciates the way in which he is always worrying about who needs him. (124, 128) Harry enjoys this new role of surrogate father better than that of middle-aged lover to a teenager. So he listens to the story of her getting into drugs, the sex in abeyance. He wonders, nonetheless, why he should always be the one to have control of himself. (188) A man has to blame himself for what happens in this human world, not God. (283) Fortunately, there is always the law, and Harry loves the law. (283, 284)

He's torn between Jill and Peggy. Jill wants him because she needs him (or any other protector/lover). She considers him a rabbit, but also a diamond in the rough. (233) Peggy wants him because she thinks he needs her. So he gives into Peggy. (274) The fire occurs while he is "locked in" with Peggy. Jill dies in the fire, and Nelson blames him for her death. (283) However, once again, as with the death of the baby, he refuses to take the blame. It was just another instance of his own bad luck. (291) Nelson thinks that once again his father has lost control. (276) Now, after the latest **catastrophe** in his life, he can't agree with Janice that love (and sex) is what makes things run. He feels there must be something else, perhaps a kind of transcendent love. (344) Janice can't see him as anything else but a prude. (345) The distance from prudishness to saintless is many light years long; Harry has no conception of "distance."

"My Janice"

Because of his extremely limited sexual contacts with Janice during those last ten years, Harry considers himself a "married saint." Besides, hasn't he let her take a sexy lover, (45, 55) who, even in the restaurant, with Harry there, sits awfully close to her? (50) Harry has never really stopped blaming Janice for the baby's death, (50) and that's why he hasn't been able to make sexual contact with her (he says). Janice feels the rejection very strongly, (55-57) and has no qualms about "shacking up" with Charlie. At her age, Harry says, she is supposed to have a good time. (58) Harry and Janice haven't made love in the light for years. (Janice was the prude at the very beginning of their relationship. Cf. *Rabbit, Run*.) When they do, Harry acquits himself quite well (three out of four), although he thinks he may have failed her again (that fourth time), even as he had been doing all along by rejecting her. (68) But that was really the baby's fault, wasn't it? (103) Now, he is ready to take Janice back, but only on those terms will he give up Jill, he tells her. (141) Janice, after all, is hot in bed; Jill is a "cool, prep-school kid applying what she knows." (132) Jill's approach works for him, but he's still ready to give her up for Janice. (152, 161)

The situation in Harry's "commune" is getting too sticky for Harry's temperament. He would welcome Janice's coming back to rescue him from Jill and Skeeter. (189) Jill has said he seems to be missing his wife, (240) a direct replay of what Ruth had said to him ten years ago. (Cf. *Rabbit, Run*) Ruth had said that the "other woman" could never prevail, because of the many hooks a wife had in a husband. Even Skeeter remarked that Harry seemed to be "all the time married," even when he was involved with another woman. (246) Harry is more broadminded now, ready to forgive (and take back) Janice. (271) They are finally together again, in the motel, and Janice wants sex. He'd like to oblige her, but what if he can't satisfy her? (349) Will this latest "rejection" impel her to run away again? He won't take the risk. (351)

Harry and Charlie

Harry knows about Charlie and Janice. He needs no headline to tell him that he is being cuckolded. (96) He can tell by the way Charlie takes over at the restaurant that he and Nelson have been relegated to the back seat. (45) When he doesn't respond to Janice's love-making overtures, Janice can't help thinking about Charlie, Charlie whose idea of a space odyssey would be "to get in the sack with your ass and ball for a week." (55) He just can't compete with Charlie as a lover, Janice tells him. If he'd been adequate, Janice admits, she would never have left him. (141) Now she knows what she had been missing all along, and she's not quite ready to give it up. Janice must have been right because Charlie is even able to get Mim, a very sophisticated dame, to go to bed with him. Harry can only imagine how it went with those two. (329) As a "playmaker," Charlie can give Harry, or any other basketball player, a run for his money.

Harry and Jill

Before Jill comes to live with him, Harry's house is an empty spacecraft "slowly spinning in the void." (92) Now this rich kid (118), who will probably test his machismo (127), is with him, and will also probably spell trouble. She begins to test him as soon as she enters the house. (130) She is uninhibited and talks about the meaning of life. "Anything that is good is in ecstasy," she tells Nelson. (143) She has many ways in which to achieve ecstasy, and Harry will be introduced to most of them, by precept or by practice. She is vaguely spiritual, and talks about God and love. (138) She also teaches Nelson how to panhandle (150), which causes puritanical Harry to slap her for trying to turn Nelson into a "beggar and a whore just like yourself." (151) But Harry will "repent" for that later on. (157)

With Skeeter's entrance into the house, both Harry and Jill will be "raped." (183) When Skeeter rings the three chime tubes to enter, the sound is probably harmonious for the last time. Harry must now share the "paternity" for Jill. She is so scared that if they don't act like big daddies to her, she may run back to dope again. (214) The paternal responsibility in ambiguous tandem with his role as a lover confuses and scares Harry. (Cf. earlier, his fear of committing incest.) He finds it hard to do both for another reason: she is a rich kid, and he has never liked rich people. (219) He should be protecting her from Skeeter's attempts to bring her back on drugs, but he doesn't. (222) He finds it increasingly difficult to react sexually to her. The "unripe hardness of her young body" turns him off. (224) The passage, by the way, contains some of the finest - and cleanest (Cf. language at top of page) - language in the novel, another possible sign that the relationship is coming to its inevitably tragic end. Jill is also confused by their relationship. Is he Daddy or Lover? (226) When he holds her in his arms, it is as if he is holding wind. (248) He knows how fragile she is, that she must be protected. Nelson pleads with him to help Jill, but his only answer is that "We can't live Jill's life for her." (255) He watches Jill and Skeeter make love and is amazed, rather than outraged. "What he sees reminds him in the first flash of the printing process, an inked plate contiguous at some few points to white paper." (260) The amorality of esthetics! See no evil is the way Harry operates, too. (288) Jill is dead now, as dead as the dead-green table and folding metal chairs in the local police station, dead, but once abundant, "as grace is abundant." (301) Mim understands how Harry felt about Jill. He likes any disaster that might set him free. "You liked it when Janice left," she says, "you liked it when your house burned down." (318) "It's too late," ill had told him not too long ago. "It's too late for you to try to love me." (263)

Harry Believes In Skeeter

The full extent of this faith that Harry has learned to have in Skeeter has been examined in the section Religious Influences.

There is only this to add: When Skeeter asks Harry if he believes that Skeeter (or someone exactly like him at some future time) is the "Christ of the New Dark Ages," Harry answers, "I do believe." (243) When Skeeter wishes to tell the full story of his "revelation," Harry says that it if happened, then "We got to deal with it somehow." (229)

Harry Redux

The big difference between the Harry of ten years ago and the Harry now is that this one has developed a "sweet funny family side" that seems to keep him worrying all the time about people who may need him. (128) Everybody agreed that the earlier Harry was a most irresponsible guy. The change, however, is somewhat specious; Harry now recognizes the need for responsibility, but he also seeks out people who can share the responsibility with him. For example, he accepts Charlie as his wife's lover because Charlie can keep his overstimulated wife under control. "Through her body, they have become brothers." (141) Skeeter, likewise, is called upon to share with Harry the paternal function toward Jill. (214) Through her body, they have become brothers in paternity. He shares with Peggy Fosnacht the sense of having been abandoned; she has also been abandoned by her spouse. They are both fasnachts, the last to be served. Since both of them have sons of about the same age, they are linked even more closely by a common "deprivation"; more importantly, Peggy as an occasional surrogate mother is able to share Harry's parental responsibility for Nelson. "Share the responsibility" is Harry's motto. If you can't take the shot at the basket yourself, pass the ball off.

In what other respects has the real Harry "returned" or been "led back"? He is now thirty-six years old and probably knows less than when he started. (28) What one hasn't done by thirty one is not likely to do, he tells his mother. He would like to live the way Mim does, but he hasn't got "what Mim has to sell." (174, 175) "As a human being I'm about C minus," he confesses to her. His rating as a husband is almost zilch. He will soon be unemployed. "Some life. Thanks, Mom." For what? For having accepted an uncreative Rabbit bringing her trophies and headlines, but nothing he had really made that was of lasting value. (84)

Still, Janice said that it was very good of him to have come back to her. (65) But she, like most of the others, no longer bothers to tell him how good he is-or, more, to the point, how good he used to be. (113) Old Tothero once said Rabbit "could slip a posse dribbling," but nobody has been that flattering lately. Babe says Harry's knuckles give her "bad vibes," he is a disaster carrier. (113) But Jill calls him an exemplary father. (136) Maybe he ought to take Jill's opinion instead of Babe's. On the other hand, the kid's ideas are too far out. He's middle-aged now, and ideas which used to grab him no longer do. "It's not that you get better ideas," he tells Jill, "the old ones just get tired." Harry is still hobbled by too many old ideas. (146) Harry still prefers a can of beer to the rhymed autobiography that Jill is reciting for him and Nelson. (154) He won't share his beer with Nelson, however, and that may be a sign that he believes (and hopes) that Nelson will find the new ideas more acceptable than he does.

But Harry listens-to Jill, to Skeeter, to Nelson. He would like to change (What can he lose?). He does, after all, set up a virtual "commune" in his own house, "a refugee camp' for one misguided white and one misguiding black. (200, 280) "It was like having two more kids in the house," he explains to the police chief. (285) Was that wrong, was that so bad for a so-called conservative? To be a Good Samaritan to two orphans, one Black, one white? Did he ever ask about color or creed? He fed them both. "I was the fucking Statue of Liberty," he tells Mim. (311) And for all that, Jill has the gall to tell him he depends too heavily on instinct rather than on reflective thought, and that when his instincts fail him, he turns cynical. (202) What was wrong with his instinct to take her and Skeeter into his house? Skeeter faults him, too: You're still cluttered up with too much common sense, and common sense just won't work. "It gets you through the days all right," Skeeter explains, "but it keeps you from knowing." (231) Knowing what? What Skeeter has been hinting at all these weeks, that "life does want death. To be alive is to kill"? (271) But Skeeter, as Harry sees him, is "religious-crazy," not "gun-crazy." (285) Nonetheless, Skeeter is right, and in the end Harry does "kill." It's all too confusing; everything moves faster nowadays-except Harry. (298) Harry likes his country (and the American way of life, 1959 style) just the way it is; if it were better, he would have to be better, and he is neither desirous of, nor capable of, being better. (153) Mutatis mutandis-with some slight changes in the setting to indicate the passing of time-Harry, if not Rabbit, is redux.

Janice Angstrom

"What we are witnessing ... is the triumph of the clitoral, after three thousand years of phallic hegemony." (Bech, 171) Now Janice can hardly be considered one of the more articulate or vigorous leaders in this women-liberating movement, but she is trying, in 1969, to find for herself a more valid identity, something Harry couldn't care less about. (98) And so she takes a lover who is both willing and able to introduce her to the delights and advantages of clitoral (and vaginal) hegemony. Harry again shows little interest in stopping her from pursuing this new identity. "She's like all you people, caught in this society," he says. "She wants to be alive while she is alive." (240)

Portrait Of Janice

Both Pop and Mom Angstrom have to tell Harry that Janice is running around with another man. Harry is not too disturbed by the news (he thinks back to his own affair with Ruth), especially since he is assured by Pop that the rumor does not claim that Janice is playing the field. (16) His moral logic tells him: a whore, no; a mistress, yes. Besides, he admits to Pop, his bed relationship with Janice hasn't been that great all these years. He has even learned to tolerate Janice's drinking, since he, too, takes a drink once in a while. (17) He has learned from Tothero (Cf. *Rabbit, Run*) that rather than let a wife become a solitary drinker (which could sometimes lead to the accidental drowning of babies), the husband should join her. (17) Still, Harry can't believe that any other man would want Janice, "that mutt." (18)

This is the new Janice, however, able to use the new permissive language without any inhibitions (38) and apparently ready to sexualize anything and everything she sees or hears. (28) Even her appearance has changed; little makeup and a face strengthened by a kind of gypsy severity have given her a plainness close to beauty. (46) Charlie has noticed this, and has exploited it to give Janice a new self-image (and agility) that have made her capable of enjoying the more "advanced" techniques of love-making. He has convinced her of how good she really is. (53) Moreover, he has done all this without sacrificing any of his own precious male dominance. Having a lover has made life for Janice one big movie. (54)

Charlie has revived the young Springer girl. (63) Janice isn't afraid to tell Harry she sleeps with Charlie, that she does things for him sexually that she would never do for Harry. Charlie is different, and she's more exciting to him than she is to Harry. "I'm sure it's just mostly our not being married," she concludes, something Harry, so expert in extramarital sex, should be able to appreciate. (64) Harry should be able to appreciate, too, that Janice is about ready to return to him. She has been a veritable tiger with Charlie, but now that she's had her "kicks for the summer," she should be permitted to return. (162) The analogy with Harry's own "summer" ten years ago with Ruth is not completely lost on him.

Janice, Run

Why does Janice run away from Harry? When she admitted that she was consorting with Charlie, she felt sure Harry would become indignant, even insulted, and fight to keep her to himself. When instead he doesn't seem to give a damn, she is outraged, and leaves to "shack up" with Charlie. (75, 80) Here again the analogy with Harry's first "flight" from Janice ten years ago (Note the **irony**: Charlie lives on Eisenhower Ave., a symbol of those other times, 1959, when a benign Eisenhower presided over a more controlled society) must not have escaped the former "runner." Harry, however, expected to come back to a more old fashioned life, and he did. (54) Two weeks later, Janice is still "in flight," having found the kind of man any woman "with fire in their crotch" would want over a "dead athlete." (97)

Harry admits that he had bored Janice, sexually and politically. (119) He had "squelched her potential." (133) He had been wholly inadequate as a bedmate. (141) He had driven her away and into the arms of Charlie. "She was desperate, fella," Charlie tells him. "Christ, hadn't you taken her to bed in ten years?" (161) Now she keeps calling Harry at the shop, complains about Jill, seems to want to come back, and sounds as if she's been drinking again. (167) That last time, ten years ago, she was also drunk, when she pleaded with him not to leave her.

Janice Redux: Mim also believes Janice wants to come back, and would, if she weren't trapped by her love for Charlie. Charlie has been the biggest thing in her life since way back when. He has helped her get out of that funk she fell into after the baby's death. She's had a taste of the "candy" in life, the freedom, the "kicks," the sensation of being a sexually aggressive woman. She's ready to give up some of the "candy," but she still wants to retain in her mind "the idea of what she's made out of the candy..." (310) And Harry has to help her, instead of saying "She can find me if she wants to." (310) Janice analyzes the extent and significance of that "candy" in terms worthy of the latest sex manual. She has learned a great deal about sex and about babies from her relationship with Charlie. (331) Now it's time for Charlie to give up his "tiger"; he's physically tired, and also afraid for his delicate heart. (332) Right now he seems to be having a heart seizure, and it's up to her to try to save him, to show Harry that she does not have "the touch of death." (335) It's time to leave Charlie while the miracle of their relationship is still fresh and palpable, before, moreover, the "tiger" kills him, even out of love. (337)

So Harry and Janice are back together again, ready to leave the house of the Springers. Janice, unlike Harry, does not wish to revert to childhood; (34) let's go to a motel instead, she suggests. They find a motel, Safe Haven, wherein Janice is all "full of sexy tricks," Harry is ready to give up sex for faith, Fort Hood for Santa Fe. (348) The subject of Jill comes up in the closing pages;

Janice wants to know whether Harry really loved the kid. "Not like I should have," he says. "She was sort of too nice." (342) He tries to convince Janice that if she hadn't run away, there would have been no Jill, no fire in the house. Janice refuses to accept the blame. "Her trip drowns babies; his burns girls. They Were Made For Each Other." (342. Capitals supplied)

Charlie Stavros

And indeed they were made for each other, as Updike has often reminded us ("Marriage is a sacrament"). The marriage is tested by giving Harry Jill; perplexed over whether he should love her or be a father to her, he manages to "kill" her, thus removing her from the scene and permitting Janice to come back consistent with her own terms. Janice is given Charlie as a lover, and within a short summer's space of time she "balls him ragged" so that he must give her up in order to survive.

"Dark and Swarthy Lover": Harry and others refer to Charlie Stavros as a "wop," a "Spaniard," almost never as an American of Greek extraction. Ironically, Harry dreams of Lyndon Johnson asking Charlie to be his Vice-President (he needs a Greek), when Charlie is diametrically and politically opposed to Spiro Agnew. (69) Indeed, Harry often can't make up his mind whether he is opposed to Charlie because Charlie is his wife's lover, or because of Charlie's "left-wing" politics.

Charlie is described as a "squarely marked-off man" (but no "square"), who moves slowly and very deliberately, "as if carrying something fragile within him" (a bad heart). Harry sees him as kind of play-maker ("making a play" for Janice?) on a basketball team, "close-set, slow, and never rattled." (44) Charlie isn't too impressed with the new technology illustrated in the film "2001-A Space Odyssey" because he doesn't find technology "that sexy." But he is grateful for the Pill, because that makes it possible for almost any girl he desires to go to bed with him. Janice, of course, has not been the first of his conquests. (62) She is flattered that he has chosen her over the many younger girls he could have had, and believes that he would even marry her, if it weren't for his bad heart. "Charlie can never marry anybody," she likes to believe. (70) And Charlie, unlike Harry, loves life, and maintains that only daylight love-making is proof of one's full appreciation of life. (71) So Janice leaves Harry for Charlie, and Babe, among others, knows full well why. Her question is rhetorical: "Honey, now what did he have you didn't?" she asks Harry, and immediately provides her own answer: "He must of had a thumb long as this badmouth's tongue." (109) Pop Angstrom thinks Charlie has ruined his daughter-in-law (an acceptable bias, since Pop is no more tolerant of "foreigners" and exotics than Harry is), but Charlie is quick to reply that he has humored, rather than ruined, Janice. (157) Nor has he ever pretended to be another "Ruth" to Janice as a "Harry." He will be no substitute spouse. (158. Note how he refuses a Daiquiri, a symbol for Ruth accepted by the reader in the earlier book.) Nor will he accept the role of seducer; Janice came running to him, he insists. (161) Moreover, it's been tough, very tough, to contain that tiger, and he is certain that it's now time to give her up. (162) He tells Janice that he has recently had sexual relations with Mim, but only three times, and that was the end of the affair. It's one of her rules, he says: three times and no more, with any man. (331) That was all just in passing. The "cage" is showing too much stress, and Janice must now give him up. "Don't lean on me, tiger," he begs her. (332) And Janice agrees; now that the stigma on her "as a giver of death" has been removed, (336) she willingly leaves him before "She might being to kill" again. (337)

Bad Heart, Good Heart: Janice had once said to Harry that if we dropped TV sets into the Vietnam jungle instead of bombs, it would be just as effective. Harry knew that it couldn't have been her own thinking, that she must have heard it from Charlie first (288-9) He was a clever one, as sophisticated about politics as he was about ordering strange foods in a restaurant. Harry wasn't quite ready to agree with Charlie's interpretation of our role in Vietnam. Charlie's talk about making Vietnam into another Japan, of LBJ's reputed offer to make North Vietnam our fifty-first state, and our endorsement of rigged elections (in Vietnam, not here; this was all before Watergate) is beginning to sound a little more plausible to Harry; but then, what does Harry know about politics? (47) Charlie must have more than a bigger "thumb" than he has, Harry is ready to admit. He's now convinced that Charlie, for a "left-wing mealy mouthed wop," is really an O.K. guy. (62) Maybe Janice's taste in lovers was not too bad after all.

Jill Pendleton

The first "linking up" of Jill and Harry is like the union of a moonchild with an earthman. (179) When he is holding her in his arms, it is as if he is "holding wind." (248) The impossibility of their relationship is the result of her own unreality, as well as his monumental stupidity. Harry can never love her because he doesn't know what she really is.

"Baby" Jill: From her very first meeting with Harry at Jimbo's, Babe senses that Jill is doomed. "That poor baby," Babe exclaims, and the reader knows at once that Jill will be the next "baby" in Harry's life. He has a sense of the impending tragedy; he sees in her "this approaching cloud, this Jill, who will be pale like the Stinger, and poisonous." But not to him, for she is a death-wish incarnate. (113) Harry has always felt guilty that he didn't get to fight in Korea. Actually, he had never had the true fighter instinct, "but now there is enough death in him so that in a way he wants to kill." (118) Babe says Harry is old enough to be Jill's father, and Harry has already "killed" one daughter. Jill is doomed. (118)

"You mustn't baby me," Jill tells Harry, as if sensing that such a role will destroy her. (125) She feels safer as Harry's lover, (226) although Harry considers her his daughter. (238) Jill is confused, moreover, because she feels like a sister to Nelson. (237) Harry also considers her a sister to Nelson, if that could be possible without her being his daughter, because Nelson "keeps losing sisters." (342) Perhaps if Harry had let Janice have that other child (it could have been another girl to replace the lost Rebbeca), Jill might have been saved from death. (33) Maybe Ruth was right in calling him Mr. Death.

"Dirty As Smoke": Harry's first glimpse of Jill at Jimbo's is of "A small white girl ... in a white dress casual and dirty as smoke." (115) It is uncertain whether this paradox of white and smoke-a white among these Blacks-hits him. He does sense in her a "perfume of class"; (116) she is Penn Park, he is Penn Villas, she is rich, he is outranked. (118) The impression of her superiority is confirmed later when she comes to live with him, and begins to cook for him in a way that renews his taste for life. "Her cooking tastes to him of things he never had; candlelight, saltwater, health fads, wealth, class." (153) She is, indeed, from another planet. (179) He also likes the fact she has run away from home. (117) If anybody can appreciate a "runner," it's Harry, the old Rabbit. Maybe it's also class that she immediately invites him to sleep with her. (128, 129) The rich always could afford freedom (of any kind) better than the poor did. And they also felt freer to experiment with all those newfangled sexual tricks than the poor did. (130, 132) Maybe that was one of the advantages of going to a prep school. Still, you have to give the rich credit for being fair: Jill's offer to sleep with him was just one of the ways in which she was expressing the Puritan ethic of "A day's work for a day's lodging." (134) Then there was that thing about her car; he had to drive a beat-up old Falcon, she had this nifty white Porsche (dirty white, of course, to indicate the present debased state of its owner). (177) Finally, there was this love affair of the rich with the Blacks, this "radical chic" (Harry, of course couldn't come up with this term himself) which led the so-called "better classes" to permit themselves to be sullied through mixing with the Blacks, and even getting hooked on drugs, as the Blacks did. (183, 236, 237) Harry can't see the drug bit for anything: sexual freedom, yes; getting hooked on drugs, no. Jill didn't have to get so angry with him for telling her about his displeasure with her drug habit. Did he love her any the less if he said that he didn't think she would stay away from drugs? (186)

"Lover Jill": Harry is no longer shocked by Jill's versatile sex practices. He's even tried a few himself, at her suggestion. (157) He can't quite agree with the reason she gives for her generosity with her "favors." "Because whatever men ask of me, I must give, I'm not interested in holding anything for myself," she says. It spooks him, because Ruth had said something similar to him ten years ago: "You make love," she said, "you try to get close to somebody." (*Rabbit, Run*, p. 155) Maybe that's why Jill drew herself as the Ace of Hearts. (233)

Fall is coming on in Pennsylvania, and Harry's desire for sex with Jill is likewise cooling off. (He is, after all, a "boy of summer.") He is "blind to the green" in Jill, to her youth; for him, summer is dying and the "flower pot red" of Brewer is returning. The thought of Brewer and its "dried blood churches" may be a symptom of the blood, the tragedy that is to come. (234) "Lover" Jill must die before "Baby" Jill does. The thought comes back to him after the tragic fire: The "apple-green ruin and the man in the green raincoat dozing on the doorstep" of his burned-down house remind him of the once-live Jill. (291) He could have, he should have, loved Jill, but "She was sort of too nice." (342) "We must be nice to her, we must be nice to the poor, the weak, the black. Love is here to stay." (138) But once again Harry has failed, first as a lover, then as a father. Jill knew the truth long before he did. "Do whatever you want with me, Harry," she said. "I can't be anything in your real life." (170) What could he do with her, a "penumbral ghost"? She was too smart, too spiritual, too classy. She kept sending out signals, but she was a player from another league. He still had that funky old style of shooting a basketball, or in living, too. (239) When he did come to realize what she was, what she might be in his life, it was too late: "it's too late," she told Harry. "It's too late for you to try to love me." (263)

Hubert "Skeeter" Farnsworth: The Sixties "saw apocalyptic criticism assimilated into middle-class culture," according to a well-known critic. Those were the years in which critics emphasized the "exhaustion, desuetude, and terminality" that were symptoms of the deathlike stasis of the Eisenhower Fifties. And, among those critics, one must certainly place the mesmeric, egomaniacal, drug-pushing, brutal Skeeter, an exponent of rational protest and revolt turned into megalomaniacal anarchy. Even as he comes to believe more and more in his destiny as the new, the all-powerful, black Jesus, he instigates **catastrophe**; but he also keeps warning the middle-class "innocents" (like Harry, for example) of the imminent death of the culture they have been defending so blindly all these years. Before he can assume the role of the Black Jesus, he is first the Black St. John, proclaiming a new - and more terrible-Apocalypse.

Skeeter the "Stinger": Fairly early in his relationship with Skeeter ("skeeter" = mosquito, of course), Harry realizes that there is something evil in this man. "He is poison, he is murder, he is black." (189) He can sting like a mosquito (187), sting like a gadfly (208), sting like a black crab. (227) Or, he can strike with the tongue of a serpent, giving out deadly venom, even as he is giving out equally deadly truth (the "seminars"). Harry might have guessed even earlier what was in store for him when he was served a Stinger instead of Daiquiri ("that lady's drink") at Jimbo's; when he saw Skeeter for the first time-a young man with a little pussy of a goatee (the sexual implications are clear) wearing silver circular, one-way glasses (he can see you, but you can't see his eyes). (107) Skeeter, they tell him, is just back from Vietnam, and that's why he's so rude, stinging with every remark he makes. (117) So rude that he rejects the hand that Harry offers him in welcoming him to his (Harry's) own house. Skeeter prefers to keep his hand "unsullied." (183) Generous Harry overlooks this rudeness and agrees to provide a refuge for this "innocent" (according to Jill) fugitive from white justice. (184) In return, Skeeter begins to "sting" Harry with all sorts of improper references to Harry's mother, Harry's God, Harry's Jesus. (187) The "stinging" becomes less offensive when it concentrates on Harry's political and social illiteracy. Strangely, Harry finds, he sleeps more soundly with Skeeter (his "conscience") in the house. (208)

Harry, however, is very much slower in comprehending the hold Skeeter has on Jill - and this is where Skeeter will instigate the **catastrophe** that will bring down Jill, the house, and Harry's whole pre-1969 concept of what life is all about. Jill sees Skeeter as a black crab, an insect-like angel with six legs, a dope-bearing, circumcised Black Jesus. (226, 227) Harry almost comprehends the peril Skeeter is threatening Jill with, and almost makes the move to pull Skeeter out of his shell into the revealing sunshine, and then hesitates; "he might get stung." (236) This is perhaps the very last chance Harry will have to save Jill. Instead, he falls for Skeeter's protestations that he is not full of hate, but of love, a dynamic force; a dynamic force, however, that does not extend to "establishment niggers" or to "radical chic" do-gooders who wish to protect them. (241) And so Harry lets Jill get hooked by her "sugar daddy," and she is eventually destroyed by him. (265) After the fire, Skeeter has a slight tinge of remorse - or is it fear? -when locked into the back of Harry's borrowed car: "Hey get in man," he says to Harry, "you're letting in the wind." (289) (Cf. 248) The black spiders have destroyed her. (259)

Skeeter as Black Peter Rabbit

It is highly probable that Harry never thought of Skeeter as a rival for Jill's body. (107, 289) In fact, Skeeter's intention from the beginning was to destroy, rather than love, her body. When Harry called Skeeter "boy," it was as one athlete calling to another, perhaps competing for the same trophy, Jill. (184) He was Skeeter's "old athlete," hesitating to accept a marijuana joint from the "boy athlete." (212) They might even be said to be sharing the "paternity" for Jill ("brothers in paternity"); she can use all the daddies she can get. No, he wouldn't turn in a "brother in paternity" to the fuzz. (235) But Skeeter is suspicious now of his honky friend, and threatens to get the whole Black Brotherhood after him "if I have to send to Philly to do it." (236) Skeeter is a "nigger" once again, (236, 238) the truce with whites is off, and he will get these two honkies to pay for their attempt to betray him. In the highly dramatic scene in which Skeeter assumes the role of the white slavemaster castigating the black girl for consorting with her black husband, he punishes Jill for ever having consorted with Harry. (244) From here on in, salvation for Jill is impossible. Her "chicken livers have burned edges and icy centers." (241)

Skeeter as Black Jesus

Skeeter was hurt in Vietnam, (232), but he apparently found God there. (230) The first impression Harry got from Skeeter's interpretation of the Vietnam War was that Skeeter was merely a radical protester who happened to be black. Then Harry started thinking that Skeeter was moving beyond revolution, even beyond violence. "... he was kind of religious-crazy," Harry tells the cop, "not gun-crazy." (285) When Jill is trying to persuade Harry to take Skeeter in, she says it's the only way to protect him from the police; "they'll crucify him." (185) The image is taken up by Harry a little later on, when he changes his mind about throwing Skeeter out: "... if he is the next Jesus," he says, facetiously, "we got to keep on His good side." (191) Harry has already been asked to accept this Black Jesus in exchange for his pansy God, his faggot Jesus. (187) But even a modern Black Jesus needs "holy books," and Jill fetches Skeeter's "library" from Jimbo's so that the "seminars" can take place later on. (201)

Harry tries to humor Skeeter about his Jesus fixation. "All Praise be Skeeter's Name," he says. "Why doncha go up to the top of Mt. Judge and have 'em [divine laws] handed to you on a tablet?" (217) Strange, but this is exactly what Harry thought he should do, about ten years earlier. (Cf. *Rabbit, Run*) Jill "accepts" Skeeter as Jesus. She even makes the point that Skeeter, like Jesus, was also circumcised. (226) And Rabbit (a less sophisticated Harry) would also recognize the Jesus in Skeeter, if only he could dispense with common sense: "I've come down ... to tell you that," Skeeter says, "since along these two thousand years somewhere you've done gone and forgotten again, right?" (231) Harry, like all the other Anti-Christs is confused. (242) Look at the Skeeter, stripped to the waist: Have you ever seen such a chest except on a crucifix? (245) And Jill, who once saw God as a giant white lily, now acknowledges Skeeter as her Lord Jesus. (262) Some "sacraments" save; others destroy.

NELSON ANGSTROM

Smaller Hands, Larger Mind

Harry has never forgiven the Springers for the hereditary shortchanging of Nelson. Nelson's small hands-Springer hands, Harry called them-would prevent him from ever becoming an athlete; and Harry still has the mistaken notion that only through athletic achievement can anybody acquire enough bliss to carry them through the later, emptier years. And so he tries to interest Nelson in sports; if not basketball, then maybe baseball. (31) To no avail; Nelson chooses to respond more readily to Jill and Skeeter, to the new morality and life style, to the new politics. Where did Harry fail the boy? By being himself, Harry. (154)

Nelson even rejects Grandfather Springer's morality. (76) He also doesn't care too much for Janice's Springer-like extravagance and taste in boys' clothes. "I told her I just wanted blue jeans," he explains to Harry. "And a Che Guevara sweatshirt, only there aren't any in Brewer." (180) Nelson is as modern as Harry is square. Harry, however, isn't quite ready to give in to the moderns. He is happy to see the flag decal is still on the back window of his old Falcon, in spite of Janice's exposure to Charlie Stavros' liberalism. (181) The kids in the neighborhood call the boy "Nigger Nellie" because he has a Black living in his house. The epithet is ironic, and doesn't quite fit the same kid who had objected to the pushy Blacks in the bus several weeks ago. (84) Still, he plays with a soccer ball put together of black-and-white pentagons of leather. Where did he stand on Skeeter and the Black Revolution, on the Vietnam war? (224) The soccer ball fits him better than the flag decal fits his father. He uses the language of sex unselfconsciously, and is well acquainted with the nature of sex. Harry feels uncomfortable about the kid's "precociousness." (135) He aims to keep his beer - and his ideas - for himself; Nelson will simply have to get his own. (154)

Brother to Jill

Nelson will get his own, and most likely with Jill's help. She reads a lot to the kid, and discusses all sorts of esoteric subjects with him. (142) At times, Harry is pleased with the brother-sister relationship that has built up between the two; (146) with the way in which she has got the kid to bathe regularly; (150) at other times, he suspects the kid is being influenced too strongly in the liberal direction, and so threatens to send him to live with his mother (and Charlie). (151)

That fateful night, when Harry and Nelson are invited to have dinner with the Fosnachts, Nelson tries to persuade Harry not to go, not to leave Jill alone with Skeeter. (269) His childlike intuition tells him death is rustling above the Angstrom house. Then again, it may be more than pure intuition; Harry and Jill had quarreled, and the incident brought back memories of that other quarrel ten years ago between Harry and Janice, which resulted in the baby's death. Would he be next? If not him, then his present "sister." (152) The news of Jill's death makes him sick. He retches, and as Harry holds the boy's head up to help him, as if from drowning, the thought comes to Harry that if he were to let go of Nelson now, this child would drown, too. (181) His "sister's" death leaves Nelson blank, apathetic, almost catatonic. He carefully studies a scrapbook he has made of the news items about the fire. (305) Harry can't reach him, and "lives with him in his parents' house as an estranged, because too much older, brother." (306) Nelson would have preferred an older sister.

Angstrom Forever

Skeeter's image of God emerging like a newborn babe terrifies Babychuck; Nelson is not that sophisticated yet. He prefers the God of his "average and ordinary" father; he even wants to grow up like Harry. (230) He would also like to see his mother come back, even if it means giving up Jill and Skeeter, and this whole exciting mess. (257) He doesn't think Harry should ever have poked fun about Janice. (217) Perhaps he might have been happier if Harry had kept his threat to send him back to Janice. (151) There is plenty of time for wisdom and enlightenment after childhood; childhood is for innocence.

MIRIAM "MIM" ANGSTROM

"If you have the guts to be yourself," Harry had once told Ruth, "other people'll pay the price." (*Rabbit, Run*, 125) Miriam has the guts, Harry doesn't. "I don't have what Mim has to sell," Harry confesses to his mother. Mim is no showboat like her brother, but in her quiet way she swings. (314) Mim is now making up for all the years she spent as a child in the shadow of Harry's glory. (325) She could have been an athlete, too, but the Rabbit beat her out-until now.

Thoroughly Modern Mim

Except for the inevitable large earrings that go back to her high-school days, Mim dresses in the style of the Sixties-loud, colorful, stripes and patches, garishly colored shoes-clownish but smart. (307) She may share many of these styles with kids under thirty, but she doesn't share their compulsions to make themselves hard and unfeeling. (314) She prefers softness, love, sex, an occasional joint; but she won't let herself become hard, like a cockroach, one of the longest surviving of all the species. (The slang term for the butt of a marijuana joint is "roach"; in Spanish, roach or cockroach is cucaracha. A careful reading of the lyrics of the song "La Cucaracha" will explain the origin of the slang term.)

Ms. Mim

Mim has an interesting explanation of the way in which she has chosen to live and of the curious types of people she has chosen to live with. Many of her "clients" are gangsters and Las Vegas-type gamblees. She sees them as puritans, living a narrow and hard life far off the straight path. They also pay for everything they get, because anything free has a fatal catch to it. That's how they survive, by the rules of the desert. And Mim - Mim is there to be paid for anything these "puritans" want of her. (312) Mim's explanation reminds Harry very much of something that Jill also believed in - "A day's work for a day's lodging." (134) Curious how the Puritan Ethic gets around! But that's about all that Mim has in common with Jill. Mim's handwriting is the old Palmer method, slant-a-cramp; Jill's has the unmistakable stamp of the private school, confident and defiant. (173) Moreover, Mim sells her sex; Jill barters it; the difference may be in the fact that Jill never lacked money - until now. Mim's philosophy is stated in still another way, in the color of the car she drives up in (indigo) and in the color of the license plates (orange on blue). (306) Blue was the color for Ruth (and for Peggy Fosnacht), for extramarital, public, or prohibited sex. Both Ruth and Peggy were whores. Orange on blue suggests sex for sale (with passion guaranteed). Mim is also a whore, but a higher-class whore. And Harry, since he doesn't have the "cash" to pay for what he wants (and must thus settle for the Ruths and the Peggys), had better settle for spending more time in his own garden and stop "hopping around nibbling at other people's." (321) He belongs with Janice; her wildness shows that she wants back in. (310) Janice is no Mim "turning ten tricks a day in Las Vegas" (90) with those Communists. (78, 59) Janice has had her little fling; Mrs. Rabbit has had her little "run," and should now settle down with Mr. Rabbit in their little hutch. Women's liberation comes in all sizes; Mim's is the large no-economy size, Janice's is the small introductory offer.

Peggy Fosnacht

Husbandless Peggy wants wifeless Harry, and makes no bones about it. Her "defense" is an "invitation." "What we most protect is where we want to be invaded." (102) Her blue bathrobe is rarely closed tight around her. Her private parts are rarely private, when Harry is near her. If he and Jill are operating on different wavelengths, she says, "Try another wavelength." (196) She offers to "heal" Harry because Harry is a warm man who has been severely hurt. "I want to help you heal," she offers, "do whatever you want with me." (197) When Harry hesitates, she reproaches him for being "chicken," for being too considerate about an ungrateful Janice. The invitation, however, remains - the open bathrobe, the visible pubic patch ... (223) Harry finally accepts Peggy's invitation to dinner. Nelson and Billy go to bed after dinner. The Daiquiris and the blue dress Peggy is wearing remind him of Ruth. He's sure of the invitation when Peggy tells him she has been doing a little whoring on the side. (271) "Wouldn't you like to cash me in?" she asks, and he does. In bed she reminds him once again of Ruth: ". . . not since Ruth has he had a woman this big." (273) Afterwards, Billy calls his mother a whore. "That's what the bridge kids say," he shouts. "You'll lay anybody." (276) Even Harry, who, that night more than any other night, should have stayed in his own briar patch, as did Skeeter. (269)

There is hope for Peggy, however, as there is for all former sinners. When Harry met Ruth in Brewer a couple of years ago, she had "gone straight," had married a farmer, and settled in Galilee. (65-66) Why Galilee? The coincidence is interesting to think about. Did Ruth proceed from whore-mother to "Mary Magdalene," to match Harry's "Jesus Christ"? Hadn't they both repented and reformed then? (Cf. *Rabbit, Run*, 292)

Mom and Pop Angstrom

Mom defends Harry at every turn and condemns Janice. She has never forgives Janice for having "tricked" Harry into marrying her. If not for Janice, Nelson wouldn't have had those "Springer hands" that prevent him from ever becoming the great athlete that his father was. (87) Harry is Hassy, the name she called him when he was a little boy. (172) Now that Harry is in trouble again with Janice, the only thing he should do is run away and save himself, to live again, to kill, if it means his own survival. (175) Janice is a dishrag and doesn't deserve to be considered. If she left him, fine. Let him be like Mim and run to freedom (149, 152) even though Harry doesn't have the same ability or guts that Mim has. Nonetheless, Harry follows him mother's advice and prays for his own rebirth. (176)

At sixty-five, Mom is dying of Parkinson's Disease. Mim can see it; (307) Pop thinks that the drug, L-dopa, is rejuvenating her. (148) But death is coming to her as sure as death is coming to Harry in the form of Jill. (149) But to the very end, Mom will defend her Harry; rules were not made for him, and so the world cannot condemn him for having broken any rules. (324) Pop is not as tolerant of Harry as Mom is; he, however, also admires Mim, and is insatiably curious about her experiences on the West Coast. Did she really work for Disney? She did; and since Disney, more than FDR, kept the United States from succumbing to Communism in the Depression, Mim is a great one, if by association only. (315)

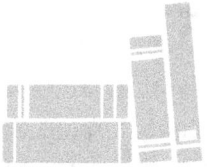

RABBIT, RUN AND RABBIT REDUX

ESSAY QUESTIONS AND ANSWERS

Question: Critics often refer to Updike as a "religious" writer, a novelist who always sets up his "intellectual-religious" scaffolding before he begins to structure his novels. To what extent is this description justified in *Rabbit, Run* and *Rabbit Redux*?

Answer: Updike has never lost the consciousness of being part of God's world, subject to His commands, eager for His grace, aware of both man's fallibility and God's forgiveness. It was a major part of his upbringing in a Lutheran home with devout parents. Even when in later years he went from Lutheranism to Congregationalism, he still retained that religious awareness that is evident in almost all his novels. Nonetheless, he makes no claim to being a theologian (although he admits to a great affinity for Karl Barth, the Protestant theologian, and has been characterized by some critics as an "unofficial" advocate of the neo-Protestantism originated by Reinhold Niebuhr), nor does he "pontificate," proselytize, or moralize. He does, however, favor strong religious figures, for example, the ministers Eccles and Kruppenbusch in *Rabbit, Run* and Skeeter in *Rabbit Redux*. One may also include the highly spiritual Jill, in the latter novel. Eccles is, of course, the representative of the Culture-Protestantism that Niebuhr was so strongly opposed to; Kruppenbusch is the **protagonist** of the traditional, orthodox Protestantism (in the form of Lutheranism) that Niebuhr was equally opposed to. Skeeter for his part can mercifully be called Evangelical (in the non-sectarian sense of the term) or independent Christian; or, less charitably, a religious fanatic or "religious-crazy" (Harry's term). In any event, it should not escape the reader's attention that Skeeter's apocalyptic, bloody approach to salvation is very close to the fire-and-brimstone manner employed by Kruppenbusch.

A quasi-religious or spiritual tone is established for *Rabbit, Run* with the Pascal quotation as epigraph: "The motions of Grace, the hardness of the heart; external circumstances." We are instantly made to understand that Rabbit is no ordinary heel, scoundrel, lecher, wife-deserter, or failed athlete; he is, rather, a soul in flight, a human being who has sinned and is constantly seeking grace. Since his own efforts are somewhat pitiful, he is assisted in his pursuit of grace by several "instruments of grace": to name a few, Eccles, Kruppenbusch, Ruth, and the "old scholar" who sells him gas during his first flight. These people (and some objects and places as well) are positioned throughout the novel like "Stations of the Cross" for Rabbit to stop at in his headlong flight into Hell.

In *Rabbit Redux*, it is Skeeter, the God-intoxicated, Jesus-type figure who tries to save Rabbit from the specious salvation he has achieved during the ten years following his final flight in *Rabbit, Run*. Since there are as many "true religions" as there are prophets or evangelists, one must assume that the salvation achieved by Rabbit earlier is now either counterfeit or out of date. Skeeter assumes that both descriptions apply, and proceeds to give "instruction" to Rabbit (and Nelson and Jill). Jill is a more impressionable catechumen, what with her advanced hippie life-style, her "liberation" from family and wealth, her use of mind-expanding "sacraments." Rabbit is almost ready to believe in Skeeter as the new Jesus, when Jill is consumed in the fire.

Neither novel is a picaresque tale of a lovable rogue or scoundrel. According to some armchair theologians (and some pulpit ones as well), Rabbit is a saint. In rebelling against the wasteland into which he is born; in consistently resisting the phony reality which he sees around him, Rabbit becomes first an absurd hero, and then, because he is so strongly dedicated to this gesture against man and his grace-less world, a saint; a saint, admittedly, it would be very difficult to include in any proper church calendar, but a saint nonetheless.

Rabbit runs, several times, but only whenever he is disillusioned by the world (or trap or net) in which he finds himself. The gesture is impulsive - he is a captive of his instincts- but it is understandable in the context of his spiritual nature. What does running make of him? A social outcast, a deserter of wife and family, a rejector of the responsibilities-hardly onerous for most of us-which life and society seem to impose on him. It is these rejections that in the final analysis emerge as part of his saintliness. He has tried to live by conventional ethics and has found them inadequate. As Rabbit and Eccles agree at one point, saints shouldn't marry.

Mindful of Updike's citing Pascal, the reader may also conclude that perhaps it is only through the action of something similar to the Christian concept of grace that a voice calls to Harry which the average man cannot hear; it is his constant running after that voice that demands of Rabbit the hardness of the heart and a definite ignorance of or obliviousness to external circumstances and consequences. Rabbit lacks grace because he has exchanged responsibility for sensuality, and has asserted his individual human independence in pride. A man without grace looks in either of two directions: to a retreat into his animal nature, or to a false reliance on his ability to reason. A man without grace is a man constantly bedeviled by anxiety; and anxiety in turn produces both pride and sensuality. A man succumbs to pride when he attributes a false significance to his marginal existence; he succumbs to sensuality when he can no longer cope with the perils and responsibilities of unlimited freedom and self-determination. Rabbit succumbs to both, and is destroyed! When he finally does accept responsibilities, in *Rabbit Redux*, he is also destroyed!

When Rabbit ceases to run (physically), but not to pursue grace, and assumes the responsibility, first, for Jill, and then for Skeeter, he is still affected with the hardness of heart suggested by Pascal. Jill tells him that people run out of fear; that they should try love for a change, instead of running. She offers him a golden opportunity to love-herself, purely, not physically. Rabbit, however, is still a slave to sensuality (fairly dormant, to be sure, until her arrival), and uses her (and Peggy, too) physically. Jill is still another "instrument of grace," but Rabbit realizes that only when it is too late.

Skeeter offers an evangel of sorts, a means of salvation through belief in him as the new Jesus, the scourger, purifier, and destroyer of all that is phony. Rabbit, so accustomed in earlier years to opposing the wasteland around him, is tempted to accept the new savior, but those few traces of a feeble rationality prevent him from accepting this new "faith." And so, the novel concludes with Rabbit having rejected love proffered by Jill, faith proffered by Skeeter, and freedom proffered by flight. Rabbit is still locked in by the hardness of his own heart.

Question: Updike has been charged with unoriginality in dealing with contemporary problems; "platitudes and stereotypes of alternative," one critic asserted-rebellion vs. conformity, the loving, passionate whore vs. the dull, drunken, respectable wife. Show how this may be true of *Rabbit, Run*. What other "stereotypes of alternative" do you find in *Rabbit Redux*?

Answer: Rabbit refuses to conform for three possible reasons: (1) he is disillusioned by the apparent phoniness of the institutions and mores around him; (2) he is too heavily dependent on instinct rather than reason or reality, and sees no reason whatsoever for abandoning his instincts; (3) he is resentful that society refuses to let him "cash in" as an adult on the reserves of glory and fame amassed as an adolescent. In all three respects, he is a less than credible or original type of rebel.

First, Rabbit's credentials as an authority on what is phony and what is genuine are fairly weak. True, he has little respect for gadgets, rejects the tackiness of modern household decor, and believes in "honest" sexual intercourse free of all impediments, especially contraceptive devices. He has tried from time to time to give up smoking and drinking because they are "unclean." He is personally fastidious - even prudish - and is critical of a Janice or a Tothero who may be guilty of sloppy "housekeeping." Nonetheless, he is, to say the least, no Holden Caulfield, and certainly no educated or informed authority on social or cultural change. Nor is he "a stranger and afraid/ In a world I never made." He refuses to conform because adult life is no game in which the conformity of team play is essential.

Secondly, Rabbit has "almost no sophisticated capacity for constructing intellectual explanations of himself and his experience." He has no answers; he knows only what "feels right." Ruth "feels right" to him; Janice does, sometimes; sometimes nothing does. On his first flight, he tries to ignore road maps and blunders into the wrong direction, never getting to the Gulf of Mexico, as he intended to. He has no confidence in the directions the old man gives him at the gas station. He is sure that, if he had trusted to his instinct, he would have made South Carolina that very evening. But he doesn't! When he runs away a second time toward the end of the novel (it may actually be the third time, if we include his flight after the nursing Janice rejects his sexual advances), it is an act of desperation, of instinct, a "flight for life," as Updike understands it. In short, because Rabbit lacks the kind of perception needed to understand why he does what he does, he must rely on instinct, on hunches, on pure animal sense, whatever that may be. In effect, it is hard to ascertain whether Rabbit makes his judgments on the basis of instinct or ignorance. He seems to be more of a retardate than a gloriously natural animal. Rabbit Angstrom as a basketball player was able to integrate his undeniably superior instinctive physical moves with the rigidly formulated rules of the game, so that right conduct was always rewarded and wrongdoing was punished. Ironically, Rabbit never fouled, or fouled out, in a basketball game; in adult life, he fouled out much too often.

Thirdly, he cannot understand how so many people around him (with the exception of Mom) could have forgotten so soon how great an athlete he used to be. "I once played a game real well," he says. "I really did. And after you're first-rate at something, no matter what, it kind of takes the kick out of being second-rate." But he is no different from all the other pathetic one-time star athletes. Ring Lardner, among other writers, has written about those "innocents" who looked upon the baseball diamond as a "surrogate spiritual environment" whose values far transcended any other values the individual players may have had. Once separated from the "surrogate spiritual environment," be it baseball diamond or basketball court, many of these same players found themselves confused, cut off from the behavioral and spiritual anchorages that had sustained them for so long. Reminiscing over past successes has little or no effect on the adult, other-oriented community. Boys will be boys, but boys cannot be adults. Rabbit as a former "boy of summer" never grew up, nor did he want to grow up. And sexual skills, extraordinary as they may be, are no substitute for the athletic skill lost. Besides, there is no crowd in the stands to applaud the sexual athlete as he successfully "shoots for the hole."

At first, Ruth is taken in by Rabbit's superior sexual skills. The reason may be that, as a whore, she is somewhat of a connoisseur of that sort of thing. The other reason may be that it is her only means of establishing what is now called a "meaningful relationship," a "morganatic marriage," as it were. Before long, she is led to believe that she is cohabiting with a "saint," a most unusual experience for a whore. But Rabbit's rare kind of saintliness requires, in fact, that he not be celibate; not if he is to implement his desire to comfort and heal through sex; it may well be that through sex Rabbit is able to see Ruth's goodness, Ruth's "heart." However, it is precisely at this point that Updike begins to work the stereotype of "the whore with a heart of gold" for all it's worth.

Ruth takes him in, cooks for him, even gets a job to help him support a second home and marriage. She even rejects several of her former "clients" who persist in calling her up on the assumption that she is conducting business as usual. Eventually, she also becomes pregnant (Rabbit had refused to let her use any contraceptive devices). Why does everybody put up with Rabbit, she wonders. Rabbit says it's because he's so lovable, so gentle. But, as Ruth knew all along, Rabbit runs back to Janice at the news that she is now in labor at the hospital. The wife always wins in the end, Ruth says, and goes back to her whoring for a while. Later on, Rabbit learns, she marries, has a few children, and "goes straight," in Galilee (Pa.). Rabbit's "fabulous phallus" has done its job; Ruth has been "healed." One simple footnote must be added, however, about the "misunderstood husband" (first stereotype), the very understanding "other woman" (second stereotype), and the non-celibate monk or saint (third stereotype). The first two stereotypes are all too familiar from English literature; the third may be found (several times) in the Decameron of Boccaccio.

Janice is no less a stereotype. She is the naive high school graduate who takes up with an older man (an ex-G.I.) in the department store where she is employed, has sexual relations with him, becomes pregnant, gets him to marry her. The next phase in her predictable career is that of the bored, sloppy housewife, addicted to TV and Old Fashioneds, pregnant again, and waiting for life to give her the signal to live again. The signal is the pathetic, accidental death of her baby, the subsequent desertion by her husband, and her "rebirth" as a woman through the sexual skills of the "other man." It is a rather maudlin version of Women's Lib, but it is consistent with the new times. For a new switch on the old situation (see above), the wife this time runs away from the husband and child and goes to live with the "other man." Now it is Charlie who is to Janice as Ruth was to Rabbit. Long live the single standard! The heady innovation proves too much for Updike ("Marriage is a sacrament, etc."), and eventually the two spouses are reunited (this time at the cost of the death of another innocent girl).

As for the other "innocent girl," we are introduced to Jill Pendleton, an upper-middle-class hippie who has run away from home after the death of her father, taken up with a group of adventurous Blacks after one unfortunate relationship with

Freddie, a seeker of God and ecstasy through drugs, and is now serving as both lover and daughter (you just can't stop admiring the ultra-modern life style) to Harry. Jill is extremely intelligent, very well read, politically advanced, and even solicitous of her new "brother," Nelson. Like Skeeter, she talks about the better life, about God, love, ecstasy, other things transcendental, and eventually succumbs to the prick of the needle. Her "immolation" makes Harry once again eligible for his wife's company, and the two middle-aged marrieds are reunited, appropriately enough, in a motel. Save for some occasionally strained analogies with the moon shots of the Sixties (Jill is, of course, a "moonchild"), Jill impresses the reader with being just another of the many thousands of "flower children" who found a temporary "pad" with some conventional member of the middle-aged, middle-American community.

Question: Updike's development as a novelist has been traced from a chronicler of middle-class domestic fierceness and its highly insignificant minicrises to an extremely competent "social secretary" (Henry James' phrase) of the broader contemporary scene. Show how the transition was effected between the two Rabbit novels.

Answer: *Rabbit, Run* was probably the definitive marriage novel of the "tranquilized Fifties," a period that marked the beginning of the decline in the belief that marriage was the foundation of everything good in our society. No divorce statistics will be cited here, but the impression persists that divorce was becoming not only more popular but easier to obtain. So was spouse-swapping and the swingers, a more tolerant attitude toward birth control and even abortion. Still, Updike was able to say in that novel that "marriage is a sacrament" and was to be preserved at all cost, even at the expense of a serious personal hell for one or both of the partners. A similar statement in *Rabbit*

Redux would probably have provoked outright disagreement or decision.

But with the Sixties, the decline in the sanctity of marriage was very noticeably accelerated. Updike himself conceded as much in his rather inferior, but enormously "liberated," novel, *Couples*, a fictional account of the burgeoning incidence of suburban adultery. Within those same ten years between Rabbit I and Rabbit II, he also wrote *Of the Farm, The Centaur*, and *Bech: A Book*, exercises in the use of very permissive, quadriliteral language, as well as in the explicit delineation of less conventional sexual practices. "I do buy Freud's notion about the radical centrality of sex," Updike admitted, even as he tried desperately - and logically - to bring Rabbit and Janice together. There is still much doubt, however, in the minds of many critics as to whether the reconciliation was effected through Updike's efforts or through the sheer exhaustion felt by Rabbit and Janice, he from his experiences with Jill and Skeeter, she from her body-expanding - and mind-expanding - relationship with Charlie Stavros.

What gave Updike the courage and the incentive to attempt such a moral quantum leap is hard to say. Not that Updike was ever a complete choir-boy type of novelist in the first place. There was low-key immorality even in his first novel, *The Poorhouse Fair*, and *Rabbit, Run* was certainly no Sunday-school romance. One possible explanation may be found in the changes in the moral climate brought about by the termination of Eisenhower's presidency, Kennedy's stylish three years, and the earthiness of Johnson's five. Then there was also the Vietnam War, America's "descent into Hell," still going on within the time frame of *Rabbit Redux*, and only recently "terminated." Add to this war as effects or symptoms the civil rights movement, the peace demonstrations on and off college campuses, the Black Revolution and the burning of cities, the post-embryonic Women's Lib campaign, the liberation of language through the Free Speech Movement in Berkeley, more widespread sexuality, pornography let loose, the drug culture, and general alienation. Updike, among many other novelists, could choose one or more of the above elements to update his novels. Indeed, he chose several. (The question before Updike and other writers is whether or not they will be able to make their next novel as permissive, in light of the June, 1973 Supreme Court decision on pornography and obscenity, and within the total retrogressive atmosphere generated by the Nixon administration. It is also likely that the novelist's prerogative has already been virtually pre-empted by Watergate, the ultimate obscenity. Updike, for one, since he is not a political novelist as such-Mailer and Roth are-may not feel up to using that event as the text for his next novel.)

The range of Updike's development as a novelist from Rabbit I to Rabbit II may be measured by examining five of the major characters who appear in one or both novels: Harry, Janice, Jill, Charlie Stavros, and Skeeter. In *Rabbit, Run*, Harry was already on the way to beer-guzzling, blue collar, suburban passivity. True, he was restless and dissatisfied, and his libido was still active enough for him to dream of mermaids under the southern sun, to retain fairly vivid memories of his glorious days as basketball star, to drop an occasional obscenity (but usually in relation to a specific sexual activity anticipated or actually involved in), and to agree readily to take up with a whore. Nonetheless, he was still a political troglodyte, rarely confused the language of the locker room with the conversational coin of the ordinary social engagement, and still firmly convinced that the right way to live was according to the precepts and tenets laid down by his former coach, Marty Tothero. By the end of the novel, he is neither chastened nor changed by the tragic event in his life, and runs away, free, for the time being.

Ten years later, we find Harry back again with Janice in their own little suburban box, a "decaying man in an American city typically run down," an ardent supporter of the Vietnam war (although part of a declining minority of such supporters), a hater of the Blacks, a defender of our national soul against the threats of an exploding pornography, and only recently weaned away from beer to Daiquiris. He is all these until-until his old world begins to change under the impetus of man's first successful attempt to land on the moon; the transmogrification of Harry is soon accelerated with Janice's desertion of him for a lover, his first direct encounter with a new breed of Blacks such as Buchanan, Babe, and Skeeter, his "adoption" of Jill, and, in due time, his "protection of bail-jumping Skeeter. From then on, it's a new Harry, brought about in his very own home. Jill reintroduces him to sex; she also introduces him to exotic foods, new literature, new ideas, and the new politics. In her presence, he finds it much easier to use so-called off-color language, and this language becomes in turn a major characteristic of the newer Updike. Whereas in the past Harry's use of four-letter words (the polite kind, that is) was an indication of the paucity of his vocabulary, now he can throw them around (the impolite kind, that is) with complete abandon, even in the presence of Janice and Nelson. Skeeter takes up Harry's re-education by introducing him to marijuana and the mysteries of Black culture; to the immorality of the Vietnam war and of the Establishment in general; to the deceptions of politics and the old religion; and to the wild possibilities of the new religion of which Skeeter will be the Black Jesus. All in all, within the short span of one summer and one fall, he is subjected to a "space odyssey" that must in the end bring about a substantial change in him. The story of his "odyssey" is the reflection of the changes that came about in Updike from Rabbit I to Rabbit II.

Janice has an even longer trip to take before she can catch up with Harry. By the end of *Rabbit, Run*, she is still the same Janice; the four years since her graduation from high school have left her the same innocent girl Harry had so easily seduced after hours in Kroll's Department Store. A mother of one and a near-mother of another, she has had no real interest in sex save what she can gather from some of the more daring commercials on TV. Her modernness doesn't extend beyond the Old Fashioneds she imbibes almost unconsciously as she imagines herself "Queen for a Day" (her favorite TV show). She is as slovenly and disorganized as the apartment she occupies. And she is deserted by her husband, not once but three times. And so the novel ends.

In *Rabbit Redux*, however, we find a new and different Janice. In ten years she has slimmed out, learned to use makeup with style, taken a steady job in the office of her father's used-car business, and acquired a lover to help overcome the neglect of her by her psychically impotent husband. Janice is now conversant not only with the techniques but with the language of advanced sexual behavior. Charlie has taught her how to sell herself to herself. She is desirable, she is his "tiger," and she cares little or nothing about her husband with the "lead gut." When he fails to react with outrage to her admission that she has a lover, she takes off (Janice, Run) to live with her lover. At this point, Janice has caught up with the Rabbit who had left her ten years ago to live with Ruth.

As in the case of Harry, Janice's emergence as a modern, independent woman parallels the changes that came over Updike the novelist from Rabbit I to Rabbit II. Had Updike not made the necessary adjustments in style, language, characterization, social and political content to accommodate the changes in our own society over a period of ten years, the new Janice would not have become visible. True, she does manifest a strong jealousy of Jill; she would come back tomorrow, if Harry told Jill to leave. But she doesn't object to Harry's carrying on with Peggy, infrequent as that actually is. And yet, when she is finally reunited with Harry, she is not at all bothered that Harry will not, or cannot, respond to her sexual needs. Rather than feel rejected, as she did during the first years after the baby's death, she feels more self-confident, ready to take on another lover (this time, hopefully, one who doesn't have a heart murmur), should Harry cut her off again from the "service" owed to a wife. Janice knows the score now.

It is fairly simple to trace the ten-year transition in Updike's development through a careful analysis of Harry and Janice, two of the characters who appear in both books. To a somewhat similar degree, Mim (who also appears in both books) may also serve to show the transition, although in *Rabbit, Run* she is already well on her way to becoming the prosperous B-girl operating on the West Coast. (See, for example, Rabbit's encounter with Mim at the Club Castanet and Ronnie Harrison's accurate evaluation of her potentialities.) The three characters new to *Rabbit Redux*, however, provide better clues than Mim: Charlie Stavros, Jill, and Skeeter. Charlie is a fairly recent social "artifact," an independent bachelor, a swinger, a political liberal, and a most available male. He doesn't seek out Janice, she seeks him out. In this respect, they are both modern: he no predator, she not ashamed to find a male partner through now-normal (she is no vamp or "hooker") means. Charlie is also modern in that he wants no long relationships, no emotional involvements. He knows that there is fun in life, and he also knows how and where to find it. Furthermore, he has a way with women, less that of the athlete coming on strong (like the younger Rabbit) and more that of the intellectual sharing a physical pleasure with a consenting woman. Charlie is of Greek extraction, and perhaps Updike is making a point here, namely that the Wasp-type lover of the Fifties has yielded to an ethnic-type lover of the Sixties. (Cf. also Skeeter and other Blacks, as the sometimes more desirable male love objects of the Sixties.)

Jill is so typical of the Sixties as to be a stereotype. She is a case study of the wild young hippie runaway who has left her affluent family to "slum around" among us less fortunate people in order to find herself. Her search for self identity leads her through the predictable maze of sex, drugs, and pious self-abasement from one strange "pad" to another. When she lands in Harry's wifeless "pad," she is ready to settle down for awhile (and this is uncharacteristic of the species) and try to re-educate this failed athlete, this oversized, cuckolded husband. She does it very simply: organic and exotic foods, books on yoga and gurus, politics of dissent, the inevitable guitar. For Harry, Jill represents not only "class," but the contemporary world that he has failed to enter after ten years of middle-American stasis. And even when she finally succumbs to drugs again, Harry is not surprised. In fact, when he does have the opportunity to save her from such a regression, he chooses not to do so. And so, she is destroyed; and the thought occurs that perhaps Harry wanted her to be destroyed, because he wasn't quite ready to live in the newer world that she represented.

Finally, it is ironic that Harry, who shared such a violent distaste for the Blacks with his father and with Nelson, provides Black Vietnam veteran Skeeter with a refuge from the police. What's more, Skeeter soon takes over the responsibility of re-educating both Harry and Nelson by conducting several seminars (without a by-your-leave from Harry) on slavery, Vietnam, the Black Revolution, and the New Gospel according to St. Skeeter. There is no doubt that Harry is permanently influenced by the "blackwashing" of his brain (he helps Skeeter get away when the authorities come looking for the bail jumper), and through him the reader is able to learn a great deal about the Black Revolution of the Sixties, an integral part of *Rabbit Redux*. The presence of Skeeter is also an index of the extent to which Updike has tried to familiarize himself with one of the most important cultural phenomena to occur during the ten years between *Rabbit, Run* and *Rabbit Redux*. This element alone could serve to show how far Updike has traveled as a novelist in ten years.

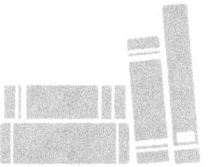

BIBLIOGRAPHY

The most complete bibliography of Updike's works is B.A. Sokoloff's *John Updike: A Comprehensive Bibliography*. Folcroft, Pennsylvania: Folcroft Press, 1972.

In listing the other works by John Updike, we have not included those titles already listed under Chronology. Note, also, that the *Uncollected Short Stories* are those published since *The Music School* collection; that many of the *Uncollected Poems* may be found in the collection *Midpoint and Other Poems*, 1969.

Uncollected Short Stories

"Marching Through Boston," *New Yorker* 1/22/66

"The Witnesses," *New Yorker* 8/13/66

"The Pro," *New Yorker* 9/17/66

"Bech in Rumania," *New Yorker* 10/8/66

"Your Lover Just Called," *Harper's* January 1967

"The Taste of Metal," *New Yorker* 3/11/67

"Museums and Women," *New Yorker* 11/18/67

"The Wait," *New Yorker* 2/17/68

"Man and Daughter in the Cold," *New Yorker* 3/9/68

"Eros Rampant," *Harper's* June 1968

"The Slump," *Esquire* July 1968

"Bech Takes Pot Luck," *New Yorker* 9/7/68

Uncollected Poems

"The Azores," *Harper's* January 1964

"Lamplight," *New Republic* 2/29/64

"Sea Knell," *New Yorker* 3/28/64

"Roman Portrait Busts," *New Republic* 2/6/65

"Postcards from Soviet Cities: Moscow; Kiev; Leningrad; Yerevan," *New Yorker* 5/29/65

"Decor, Poem," *American Scholar* Summer 1965

"Home Movies," *New Republic* 1/8/66

"The Lament of Abrashka Tertz, A Russian Song Rendered by John Updike," *New Leader* 1/17/66

"Elm," Polemic Winter 1966

"Antigua," *New Yorker* 2/11/67

"Subway Love," *New Republic* 5/20/67

"Angels," *New Yorker* 1/27/68

"The Naked Ape," *New Republic* 2/3/68

"The Origin of Laughter," *Atlantic Monthly* June 1968

"Topsfield Fair," *American Scholar* Summer 1968

"America and I Sat Down Together," poem by Yevgeny Yevtushenko, translated by John Updike and Albert C. Tood, *Holiday*, November 1968

"Report of Health," *New Yorker* 2/22/69

"Cunts," *New York Quarterly*, Summer 1973

Uncollected Essays

"Death's Heads," "Books," *New Yorker* 10/2/65

"The Author as Librarian," "Books," *New Yorker* 10/30/65

"The Fork," "Books," *New Yorker* 2/26/66

"The Mastery of Miss Warner," *New Republic* 3/5/66

"Two Points on a Descending Curve," "Books," *New Yorker* 1/7/67

"Nabokov's Look Back: a National Loss," *Life* 1/13/67

"Behold Gombrowiczs," "Books," *New Yorker* 9/23/67

"Grove Is My Press, and Avant My Garde," "Books," *New Yorker* 11/4/67

"My Mind Was Without a Shadow," "Books," *New Yorker* 12/2/67

"Questions Concerning Giacomo," "Books," *New Yorker* 4/6/68

"Letter from Anguilla," *New Yorker* 6/22/68

"Indifference," "Books," *New Yorker* 11/2/68

"Jong Love," "Books," *New Yorker* 12/17/73

General Criticism

Aldridge, John W. "The Private Vice of John Updike," *Time to Murder and Create: The Contemporary Novel in Crisis*. New York: McKay, 1966. Updike's "private vice" is that he overwrites (Mailer thinks it's because Updike cannot handle plot too well), and his major characters are stereotypes: Rabbit is the all-American heel, Ruth is the whore with a heart of gold, etc.

De Bellis, Jack. "The Group and John Updike," *Sewanee Review*, 72 (Summer, 1964). John Updike as maverick.

Detweiler, Robert, "John Updike and the Indictment of Culture-Protestants," *Four Spiritual Crises in Mid-Century American Fiction*. Gainesville: University of Florida Press, 1964. Updike has always admitted that he's an ardent follower of Karl Barth. According to Detweiler, he is also a vigorous supporter of Reinhold Niebuhr, rooting for a return from reason to faith.

Doyle, P.A. "Updike's Fiction: Motifs and Techniques," *Catholic World*, 199 (September, 1964). The importance of grace and other redemptive elements in Updike's God-centered world.

Finkelstein, Sidney. "Acceptance of Alienation: John Updike and James Purdy," *Existentialism and Alienation in American Literature*. New York: International Publishers, 1965. Updike's heroes are existential rather than neo-Protestant.

Galloway, David D. "The Absurd Man as Saint: The Novels of John Updike," *The Absurd Hero in American Fiction: Updike, Styron, Bellow and Salinger*. Austin: University of Texas, 1966. The argument once again that Updike is no Culture-Protestant but a firm believer in Niebuhr.

Geismar, Maxwell, "The American Short Story Today," *Studies on the Left*, 4 (Spring, 1964). A more secular interpretation of Updike, as well as an explication of the way in which Updike converts some of his best short stories into novels.

Hamilton, Alice. "Between Innocence and Experience: From Joyce to Updike," *Dalhousie Review*, 49 (Spring, 1969). Peter Caldwell and Rabbit Angstrom share some, but not too many, of the characteristics of Stephen Dedalus.

Hamilton, Kenneth. "John Updike: Chronicler of the Time of the Death of God," *Christian Century* (June, 1967). A brief restatement of the thesis held by Detweiler and Galloway (see above).

Hamilton, Alice and Kenneth. *John Updike: A Critical Essay* (later expanded into a more comprehensive book entitled *The Elements or John Updike*). Grand Rapids (Mich.): Eerdmans, 1967.

Harper, Howard M., Jr. "John Updike," *Desperate Faith - A study of Bellow, Salinger, Mailer, Baldwin and Updike*. Chapel Hill: University of North

Carolina Press, 1967. In Updike, the greater emphasis is on faith; in the others, on despair and the need for violence.

Hicks, Granville. "Generations of the Fifties: Malamud, Gold, and Updike," *The Creative Present*, eds. Nona Balakian and Charles Simmons. New York: Double-day, 1963. The differences between the two Jewish writers and the Protestant Updike are minimized as Updike's common sharing of the newer techniques of realistic fiction is emphasized.

"Mysteries of the Commonplace," *Saturday Review*, 45 (March 17, 1962). Updike as the chronicler of the "little man" and the trivia of everyday existence.

Howard, Jane. "Can a Nice Novelist Finish First?" *Life* (November 4, 1966). How can a compassionate Updike compete with the more ruthless writers today?

Kauffman, Stanley. "Onward with Updike," *New Republic*, 155 (September 24, 1966). Updike once again is taken to task for his very affirmative attitude toward life. Does this interfere with his ability to report the contemporary scene faithfully and realistically? Kauffman thinks it does.

LaCourse, Guerin. "The Innocence of John Updike," *Commonweal*, 77 (February 8, 1963). Nobody has ever accused Updike of being innocent or unsophisticated; however, he does enjoy underlining the innocence of his characters.

Mizener, Arthur. "The American Hero as High-School Boy: Peter Caldwell," *The Sense of Life in the Modern Novel*. Boston: Houghton Mifflin, 1964. Peter is a direct descendant of Rabbit I; Rabbit II is a direct descendant of Peter. Both Rabbits are a study in arrested adolescence.

Muradian, Thaddeus, "The World of Updike," *English Journal* LIV (October, 1965). Some interesting observations on the post-Pennsylvania Dutch generation Updike writes about.

Nichols, Lewis. "Talk with John Updike," *New York Times Book Review* 73 (April 7, 1968). Why Johnny Can Write and Write and Write . . .

Novak, Michael, "Updike's Quest for Liturgy," *Commonweal* 78 (May 10, 1963). Until Updike himself makes a public disavowal of same, certain critics will persist in claiming that all of Updike's novels are religious parables.

O'Connor, William Van. "John Updike and William Styron: The Burden of Talent," *Contemporary American Novelists*, ed. Harry T. Moore. Carbondale: Southern Illinois University Press, 1964. In Updike's case, the man is certainly the style, and the style is the man. Updikes' preoccupation with style to the detriment of sense is examined.

Podhoretz, Norman. "A Dissent on Updike," *Doings and Undoings: The Fifties and after in American Writing*. New York: Farrar, Straus and Giroux, 1964. Mainly a dissent on *The Centaur*.

Rupp, Richard H. "John Updike: Style in Search of a Center," *Sewanee Review* LXXV (Autumn, 1967). The argument is better stated by O'Connor (see above).

Samuels, Charles Thomas. "The Art of Fiction, XLIII: John Updike," *Paris Review*, 45 (Winter, 1968). Informative, right out of the rabbit's mouth. Updike, frank and charming.

Updike, John. "Writers I have Met," *New York Times Book Review* 73 (August 11, 1968). It could have been an equal time" situation in which Updike would have answered his critics; instead, some very cogent observations on some of Updike's contemporaries.

Wyatt, Bryant N. "John Updike: The Psychological Novel in Search of Structure," *Twentieth Century Literature* XIII (July 1967). Updike himself rarely refers to his novels as "psychological," nor does he admit to an absence of structure in them. The structure in his novels, while not so rigid as that in a Jamesian novel, is not so loose as that in some of the more recent novels.

Yates, Norris W. "The Doubt and Faith of John Updike," *College English*, 26 (March, 1965). Because Updike has admitted to being a regular churchgoer (Is this sinful in a novelist?) he must accept every other critic's contention that he (Updike) is a "religious" writer. Another commentary on Updike's possible rejection of Culture-Protestantism in favor of a full return to faith.

Criticism of "Rabbit, Run"

Note

Where certain titles are repeated from the General Criticism list, specific page numbers are given wherein material on *Rabbit, Run* is generously provided.

Alley, Alvin D., and Hugh Agee. "Existential Heroes: Frank Alpine and Rabbit Angstrom," *Ball State University Forum* IX (Winter, 1968). In Malamud's *The Assistant*, Frank Alpine settles for a religious solution; in *Rabbit, Run*, Rabbit Angstrom rejects such a solution and runs away.

Brenner, Gerry. "*Rabbit, Run*: John Updike's Criticism of the 'Return to Nature,'" *Twentieth Century Literature* XII (April, 1966).

Detweiler, Robert. *Four Spiritual Crises in Mid-Century American Fiction*, 14-24. How Rabbit translated feeling into sensuality, then into sexuality, then into nothingness, and so lost the chance to achieve grace.

Doner, Dean. "Rabbit Angstrom's Unseen World," *New World Writing*, 20 (1962) Rabbit's several "visions," or how to escape the thousand and one traps society sets for a free soul.

Duncan, Graham T. "The Thing Itself in *Rabbit, Run*," *English Record*, 13 (September, 1964). An academically philosophical approach to Rabbit's dilemma, or from Kant to Existentialism.

Finkelstein, Sidney. *Existentialism and Alienation in American Literature*, 244-246. Not all instances of alienation lead to Existentialism.

Galloway, David D. *The Absurd Hero in American Fiction*, 27-40. How an absurd hero can actually be a secular saint.

Hamilton, Alice and Kenneth. *John Updike: A Critical Essay*, 31-36. On the "parable" of Peter Rabbit.

Harper, Howard M., Jr. *Desperate Faith*, 165-173. More on the making of a "latter-day saint."

Hertzel, Leo J. "Rabbit in the Great North Woods," *University Review* XXXIII. (December, 1966). How much "rabbit" is there in Harry, how much "man" is there in rabbit?

Standley, Fred L. "*Rabbit, Run*: An Image of Life," *Midwest Quarterly* VIII (Summer, 1967). Rabbit Angstrom is not that atypical of the contemporary human condition.

Stubbs, John C. "The Search for Perfection in *Rabbit, Run*," *Critique* X (November 2, 1968). Rabbit's perfect world of organized athletics as opposed to the meretricious world of gadgets and synthetics.

Tate, Sister Judith M. "John Updike: Of Rabbits and Centaurs," *Critic*, 22 (February-March, 1964). Which is preferable: half-man, half-rabbit, or half-man, half-horse? Perhaps Lemuel Gulliver might be the most qualified to decide.

Walcutt, Charles Child. "The Centripetal Action: John Updike's The Centaur and *Rabbit, Run,*" *Man's Changing Mask: Modes and Methods of Characterization in Fiction*. Minneapolis: University of Minnesota Press, 1966. From the anthropomorphic treatment of certain animals by the Greeks to the more modern, Yeatsian use of masks.

Criticism of "Rabbit Redux"

Aldridge, John W. "Askew Halo for John Updike," *Saturday Review*, June 27, 1970. Aldridge doesn't "buy" Updike's "spirituality"; nor does he care for the stereotypical and clichéd manner in which Updike reports the present scene.

Broyard, Anatole. "All the Way with Updike," *Life*, June 19, 1970. Updike's "space odyssey" exhilarates with its awareness of the "now" thing of space exploration and the new life styles.

Burchard, Rachael C. "John Updike: Yea Sayings," *Crosscurrents*, 1971, Southern Illinois University Press. One vote for Updike's positive view of life, for his counterthrust to the nihilism rampant today.

Kazin, Alfred. "O'Hara, Cheever and Updike," *New York Review of Books*, April 19, 1973. Updike once again putting up "his usual intellectual-religious scaffolding" to examine the subject of suburban marriage.

Samuels, Charles T. "John Updike," *Pamphlets on American Writers*, Series 79, University of Minnesota Press, 1969. A possible updating of Updike in light of *Rabbit Redux*.

Taylor, Larry E. "Pastoral and Anti-Pastoral Patterns in John Updike's Fiction." *Crosscurrents*, 1971, Southern Illinois University Press. From the farm to the suburb: a history of lost innocence.

Updike: John. "First Lunar Invitational," *New Yorker*, February 27, 1971. An obvious "plug" for *Rabbit Redux*, but also prophetic in that it may have been written before Alan Shepard took his now-historic golf-club swing on the moon (Feb. 5, 1971).

www.ingramcontent.com/pod-product-compliance
Lightning Source LLC
LaVergne TN
LVHW011709060526
838200LV00051B/2828